have you
eaten?

BILLY LAW

have you eaten?

hardie grant books

MELBOURNE · LONDON

What's INSIDE?

I AM WHAT I ATE {9}

IN MY KITCHEN {278}
INDEX {282}

拆了芝丹往
毁了茨厂街
没了唐人街

I AM what I ate

I was born in Ipoh, Malaysia, and come from a family of eight. Even with so many mouths to feed, there was never a shortage of food on our table at dinner, with Mum preparing up to six dishes each night. Dinner time was always my favourite time of the day; the family sitting together over a meal, sharing the events of our daily lives with each other. Whenever my mum cooked a whole fish, my dad would usually go for the head, my sisters preferred the no-bones meaty part, while my second brother and I would fight for the crispy fish tail. It's these small things, this ability to connect with one another through our food, that defines the unity in our family.

Many Malaysians never really think themselves as 'foodies' because food simply runs in our bloodstreams, and eating six times a day in this food-obsessed country is considered quite normal. For me, a day's meal could include wonton noodle soup for breakfast followed by a light fruit snack to beat the tropical heat, then Hainan chicken rice for lunch, Malay kuih (cake) for afternoon tea, Mum's cooking for dinner, and then a midnight snack with friends at a local mamak stall for hawker food: satay skewers, ice kachang and roti canai. I love food in all its amazing variety and I believe we should try everything once, love it or hate it. But when it came to cooking, that was another story...

NEVER TOO LATE

My cooking history is pretty boring and definitely not as nostalgic when compared to others. There are no stories of me as a kid spending time in the kitchen cooking with my mum, nor are there any recipes that have been handed down from my mum or my grandma to me. Occasionally, I was asked to help roll peanut butter cookies during Lunar New Year or to pound the chilli paste in a mortar and pestle, but that's as far as my cooking duties went. Even though we never helped much in the kitchen, I still liked to watch my mum cook, observing the ingredients as she threw them into the wok, how she seasoned dishes just by guess, the way she chopped a whole chicken or fried a whole fish — I was fascinated by it all.

I actually didn't pick up a spatula and a wok until I was nineteen, when I moved to Australia in 1996 to further study Computer Science. Like any poor uni student, the only way to survive the hunger pangs was to start cooking. I still remember the first dish that I cooked for my housemates: honey and soy-glazed chicken wings. And, believe it or not, that was the first time I ever touched cold raw meat with my bare hands! Thankfully, the dish was a hit but, more importantly, it was my first baby step towards discovering my love of cooking.

COOKING UP A STORM

Fast forward 15 years later, and I suddenly found myself cooking for Gary Mehigan, George Calombaris and Matt Preston as part of the TV cooking show MasterChef Australia. I had never imagined, not in a million years, that I'd be cooking in front of cameras while millions of Australians were glued to the TV watching me.

It was a gruelling six months' experience, yet also the most rewarding one in my cooking journey thus far. I feel incredibly grateful and humbled to have met people on the show that I greatly admire, including Heston Blumenthal, René Redzepi, Anthony Bourdain, Maggie Beer, David Chang, Marco Pierre White and Nigella Lawson, to name just a few. And, not to forget to mention the opportunity of meeting and cooking one of my favourite vegetarian dishes for his holiness, the Dalai Lama. This was a money-can't-buy experience that I will cherish forever.

Then there were the other 23 contestants that I met in the MasterChef house. Despite the fact we were all competing against each other, we found ourselves helping one other in the kitchen, sharing cooking tips and supporting each other throughout the whole process — bonded by our love of good food.

HAVE YOU EATEN?

But before MasterChef, many may already know me as Billy, the food blogger behind A Table For Two (www.atablefortwo.com.au). I've been writing my blog for over 4 years now, and it is a great way for me to share my recipes, dining experiences and occasional travel stories with anyone who is interested. Through my food blog and my involvement in MasterChef, a whole new culinary door opened for me, and I was very lucky to meet so many talented people in the industry, including my friend Paul from Hardie Grant Books. When he approached me with an opportunity to write a cookbook, I immediately jumped at his offer!

In the beginning it was all a blur, and I had to keep pinching myself to make sure it wasn't a dream. Even though I didn't have a theme for the book and nor did I know what recipes I wanted to write, I already had the perfect title in mind. In Malaysia, it is quite common for Malaysians to greet each other saying, 'Have you eaten?' instead of the usual, 'Hey, how are you?' I simply couldn't think of anything more appropriate for the title of a cookbook that reflects my background, my culture and my food.

Have You Eaten? is a book for those who love cooking and want to learn more, and for those who want to get a little bit more creative in the kitchen. There is something for everyone, from easy peasy weeknight meals to fancy dinner party dishes. Some of the recipes may look daunting and complicated, but I've written them so you can pull them apart into smaller recipes that can be easily achieved. You will also find some of the components in some recipes can be adapted to other dishes in the cookbook.

I truly believe there are no fixed rules in cooking. Once you have grasped the basic theories of flavours and texture matching, the possibilities are endless and that's what makes cooking so enjoyable!

So, have you eaten?

CHAPTER 1

Black pudding Scotch quail egg sliders ✦ GRILLED PROSCIUTTO-WRAPPED FIGS WITH CHÈVRE, ALMOND & HONEY ✦ Sweet caramelised onion & feta tartlets ✦ BRIE EN CROUTE WITH CRANBERRIES & WALNUTS ✦ Holy moly guacamole! JAMÓN CROQUETTES WITH ROMESCO SAUCE ✦ Zing beneath my wings ✦ FIVE-SPICED DUCK PANCAKES ✦ Chicken liver parfait ✦ GUINNESS BATTERED PRAWNS ✦ Pandan chicken ✦ OYSTERS WITH CUCUMBER SORBET & PEPPER SPRAY ✦ Grilled tuna jaw with teriyaki glaze ✦ OTAK-OTAK PANGGANG {GRILLED SPICY FISH PASTE IN BANANA LEAF} ✦ Chorizo & prawn skewers

APPETISER, STARTER, SNACK — WHATEVER YOU WANT TO CALL IT, FINGER FOOD IS THE PERFECT ICE-BREAKER AT ANY COCKTAIL OR DINNER PARTY. THESE ARE SOME OF MY FAVOURITE RECIPES TO HELP GET THE PARTY STARTED.

BLACK PUDDING
Scotch quail
EGG sliders

MAKES
10

10 quail eggs
200 g (7 oz) black pudding
2 good-quality pork sausages,
  skinned
pinch of salt
½ teaspoon ground black
  pepper
75 g (2½ oz/½ cup) plain
  (all-purpose) flour
2 eggs, lightly beaten
60 g (2 oz/1 cup) panko
  crumbs
vegetable oil, for deep-frying
10 mini bun rolls, halved and
  lightly toasted
Wasabi mayo (page 270)
10 cornichons

I ALWAYS ENCOURAGE
MY FRIENDS TO TRY
SOMETHING THEY'VE
NEVER EATEN BEFORE, AND
OFTEN THE ONLY WAY TO
DO THIS IS TO TRICK THEM
A LITTLE. A LOT OF PEOPLE
PROBABLY AREN'T TOO KEEN
ON THE IDEA OF EATING
CONGEALED PIG'S BLOOD,
BUT I HAVE TO ADMIT THAT
I DO HAVE A SOFT SPOT
FOR BLACK PUDDING — OR
BLOOD SAUSAGE AS IT'S
SOMETIMES CALLED. I'VE
MADE THESE WHIMSICAL
MINI SCOTCH EGG SLIDERS
(THREE-BITE-SIZED
BURGERS) USING QUAIL
EGGS, WHICH ARE WRAPPED
IN A MINCED MIX OF BLACK
PUDDING AND SAUSAGE
MEAT, THEN CONCEALED
IN A CRUNCHY BLANKET
OF PANKO CRUMBS. I JUST
DON'T TELL THEM WHAT'S
INSIDE THE SCOTCH EGG
UNTIL THEY HAVE FINISHED
EATING IT. SHHH ...

1 Fill a small saucepan with water and bring to the boil over high heat. Once the water is on a rolling boil, carefully drop the quail eggs into the water and cook for 1 minute. Ladle the eggs out and quickly dunk them into a bowl of iced water to stop the cooking process. Peel the eggs carefully and set them aside.

2 Put the black pudding in a small food processor and process until crumbly. Put the black pudding and sausage mince in a mixing bowl, season with the salt and pepper and mix together until well combined. Scoop a heaped tablespoon of the mince and, with cleaned hands, roll it into a ball, then flatten it into a disc in the palm of your hand. Place a quail egg in the centre, wrap the mince over the egg, making sure the egg is fully sealed inside, then roll it back into a ball and place on a tray. Repeat the process until all the mince and eggs are used.

3 Prepare 3 separate bowls of flour, beaten egg and panko crumbs, ready for coating. Roll each mince ball in flour, shake off any excess, then dip it in the beaten egg, making sure it is fully coated, and then finally roll it in the panko crumbs. You can coat the ball twice in beaten egg and panko crumbs for a better crust. Repeat with the rest of the mince balls. Refrigerate for 30 minutes before frying.

4 Pour the vegetable oil into a medium saucepan until about one-third full, then heat the oil to 190°C (375°F) over medium–high heat. Test to see if the oil is hot enough by dipping a wooden chopstick into the hot oil — if the oil starts steadily bubbling around the chopstick, it's ready. Working in batches, deep-fry the scotch eggs for 3 minutes, or until golden brown, remove with a slotted spoon and drain on paper towel.

5 To serve, put a dollop of wasabi mayo on the bottom halves of the buns, top with a scotch egg, then cover with the bun tops. Use a toothpick to secure a cornichon on top of each slider.

Grilled PROSCIUTTO-WRAPPED FIGS with chèvre, almond & honey

SOMETIMES THE SIMPLEST FOOD CAN BE THE MOST GRATIFYING. THIS DISH IS A GOOD EXAMPLE: SWEET SYRUPY HONEYED FIGS AND SHARP GOAT'S CHEESE WRAPPED IN CRISPY PROSCIUTTO. NEED I SAY MORE?

12 ripe figs
6 strips prosciutto,
    cut in half
    lengthwise
12 toothpicks
20 g (¼ oz) chèvre
    (goat's cheese)
20 g (¼ oz) butter
4 tablespoons honey
handful of almond
    flakes

1 Preheat the oven to 240°C (460°F). Remove the stalks on the figs, then cut them into quarters, starting from the top and cutting only halfway down, leaving the base intact. Using both thumbs and index fingers, gently squeeze the base of the figs to open them up.

2 Wrap each fig with a slice of prosciutto and secure it with a toothpick. Stuff each fig with a teaspoon of chèvre, then place on a baking tray. Put a small knob of butter on top of the figs, drizzle with the honey and then sprinkle over the almond flakes. Place the figs on the top rack in the oven and bake for 10 minutes, or until the figs are scorched a little and the prosciutto is slightly crisp.

MAKES
12

Sweet CARAMELISED ONION & FETA tartlets

80 g (3 oz) butter
2 large brown onions, thinly sliced
1 tablespoon sugar
pinch of salt
2 tablespoons white wine (see note)
3 sprigs thyme, leaves picked
200 g (7 oz) feta cheese

SAVOURY PASTRY

150 g (5 oz/1 cup) plain (all-purpose)
  flour
50 g (2 oz) chilled butter, cut into cubes
pinch of salt
3 tablespoons chilled water

1 To make the savoury pastry, put the flour, butter and salt into a food processor. Using the pulse button, process until the mixture resembles fine crumbs. While still processing, slowly add the water to the mixture in a steady stream, until the mixture comes together to form a dough. Turn out onto a lightly floured work surface and flatten the dough into a disc, then wrap in plastic wrap. Place the dough in the refrigerator to rest for at least 30 minutes.

2 Preheat the oven to 170°C (340°F). Place the dough on a floured work surface and roll it out to a 3 mm ($\frac{1}{8}$ inch) thickness. Use an 8 cm ($3\frac{1}{4}$ inch) cookie cutter to cut the dough into discs, then line a 24-hole mini tart tin with the pastry. Transfer the tin to the refrigerator and let the pastry set for 20 minutes. Remove and prick the pastry bases a few times with a fork. Blind bake the tart cases for about 12–15 minutes, or until golden brown. Remove from the oven and set aside to cool a little, then take the pastry cases out of the tin and rest on a wire rack until completely cool.

3 To caramelise the onions, melt the butter in a saucepan over medium–low heat. Add the onions, sugar and salt and sauté for about 35–40 minutes, or until the onions are softened and golden brown. Stir frequently so the onions don't catch on the pan and burn. When the onions are soft, deglaze the pan with the wine, add the thyme leaves and cook until all the liquid has evaporated. Set aside to cool.

4 Turn the oven back to 170°C (340°F). Fill the tart cases with the caramelised onion, then top with the feta. Bake for 10 minutes, or until the cheese has melted slightly and is lightly golden on the top.

Note: To deglaze the pan, you can use white wine, red wine, brandy, stock or even water.

MAKES
ABOUT
20

WHO'D HAVE THOUGHT THAT SIMPLY COOKING ONIONS FOR A LONG TIME WOULD RENDER THEM SO DELICIOUSLY SWEET? IF YOU ARE GOING TO MAKE CARAMELISED ONION, I'D SUGGEST YOU MAKE A BIG BATCH, AS IT'S SO VERSATILE — USE THE ONIONS ON PIZZA, IN PASTA, STUFFINGS AND, OF COURSE, WITH YOUR NEXT SAUSAGE SIZZLE.

FOR THIS RECIPE I LOVE THE COMBO OF SWEET CARAMELISED ONION WITH BRINED FETA CHEESE, WHILE THE BUTTERY PASTRY SIMPLY CRUMBLES AND MELTS IN THE MOUTH. IT IS A LITTLE EXTRA EFFORT TO MAKE YOUR OWN PASTRY BUT, TRUST ME, IT'S WELL WORTH THE EFFORT.

Brie EN CROUTE with CRANBERRIES & WALNUTS

2 bacon slices, cut into thin strips

30 g (1 oz/¼ cup) walnuts, toasted then roughly chopped

30 g (1 oz) dried cranberries, roughly chopped

2 tablespoons honey

1 sheet puff pastry

plain (all-purpose) flour, for dusting

200 g (7 oz) double brie cheese wheel

1 egg, lightly beaten for egg wash

crackers or lavosh bread, to serve

1 Heat a frying pan over medium heat and fry the bacon strips until browned and crispy, then remove and drain on paper towel. Put the fried bacon, walnuts, cranberries and honey into a bowl and mix well.

2 Preheat the oven to 200°C (400°F). Lay the sheet of puff pastry (make sure it is still cold but malleable) on a floured surface and dust the pastry with flour so it doesn't stick, then roll it out to about 35 cm (14 inches) square. Place the brie on top, positioning it near one of the pastry corners. Using a pizza cutter or sharp knife, cut out a pastry circle around the brie, leaving a 5 cm (2 inch) border. Save the pastry offcuts for later.

3 Pile the bacon and walnut mixture on top of the brie. Working in a clockwise direction, lift up one section of the pastry and fold it over to cover the side of the brie, then lift up the next section of pastry and drape it over the previous fold. Repeat until all sides of the brie are covered with pastry, except the top.

4 Roll out the largest pastry offcut a little wider, then cut it out using the round lid that comes with the cheese as a guide, or a 10 cm (4 inch) round cookie cutter. Place the pastry round on top of the brie, and seal the pastries by crimping along the edges using a fork. Decorate the brie with the remaining offcuts, then brush all over the pastry with the egg wash.

5 Place the pastry-wrapped cheese on a baking tray lined with baking paper and bake for 25 minutes, or until the pastry is puffed and golden brown. Let it cool for 20 minutes before serving. If you want the cheese to be a little less gooey, then let it rest for 1 hour. Serve with the crackers or lavosh bread.

SERVES
4

THERE IS NOTHING BETTER THAN CUTTING THIS DOME OF GOLDEN PASTRY OPEN AND UNLEASHING A RIVER OF MOLTEN CHEESE. MAKE SURE YOU HAVE CRACKERS READY TO SCRAPE UP ALL THE CHEESY GOODNESS. SINCE WE ARE GOING TO BAKE AND MELT THE CHEESE, SINGLE OR DOUBLE BRIE WILL DO JUST FINE. YOU CAN ADD A FEW CRANBERRIES OR CHERRIES AND SERVE THIS AT CHRISTMAS, OR SIMPLY STUFF THE BRIE WITH A FEW GARLIC CLOVES AND THYME LEAVES.

AS FAR AS DIPS GO IT'S HARD TO BEAT A GREAT GUACAMOLE, AND IT IS ONE OF THE EASIEST RECIPES TO WHIP UP FOR UNEXPECTED GUESTS. EVERYONE HAS THEIR OWN SECRET RECIPE FOR A GOOD GUACAMOLE, AND THIS IS MY VERSION, SERVED WITH PORK SCRATCHINGS. NOT FOR THE FAINT-HEARTED!

HOLY MOLY
guacamole!

3 ripe avocados,
  halved, stones
  removed
dash of Tabasco
  sauce
juice of 1 lime
½ red onion, diced

2 roma (plum)
  tomatoes, seeded
  and diced
handful of coriander
  (cilantro) leaves,
  roughly chopped
1 garlic clove, minced

½ teaspoon sea salt
cayenne pepper,
  to taste
1 packet of pork
  scratchings
  (see note)

1 Use a spoon to scoop the avocado flesh into a mixing bowl. Add the Tabasco sauce and lime juice, then use a fork to mash it well. Fold in the onion, tomato, coriander and garlic. Season with the salt and give it a quick mix.

2 Transfer the guacamole into a serving bowl and sprinkle a pinch of cayenne pepper over the top. Serve with a bowl of pork scratchings sprinkled with a little extra cayenne pepper.

Tip: *To avoid the guacamole turning brown from oxidation, it is best to make it just before guests arrive. If you do prefer to make it ahead of time, cover with plastic wrap and leave in the refrigerator for no longer than 2 hours.*

Note: *Pork scratchings, or pork crackles, are available at Asian or European grocers. A 300 g (10¼ oz) packet is sufficient for this recipe.*

SERVES
A
CROWD

Jamón croquettes with ROMESCO SAUCE

JAMÓN IS DRY-CURED HAM, SLICED PAPER THIN, AND IS THE CULINARY SYMBOL OF SPAIN. THE TWO PRIMARY TYPES ARE JAMÓN SERRANO, WHICH IS THE MORE COMMON CURED HAM FROM WHITE PIGS, AND JAMÓN IBÉRICO, FROM IBERIAN BLACK PIGS, WHICH HAS A BETTER QUALITY AND RICHER FLAVOUR. THESE JAMÓN CROQUETTES ARE EASY TO MAKE, BUT IF YOU'RE ENTERTAINING, IT'S BEST TO MAKE THE ROMESCO SAUCE AND HAVE THE CROQUETTES ROLLED OUT THE DAY BEFORE, THEN ALL YOU HAVE TO DO IS DEEP-FRY THEM.

80 g (3 oz) butter
½ brown onion, finely diced
75 g (2½ oz/½ cup) plain (all-purpose) flour
500 ml (17 fl oz/2 cups) full-cream milk
100 g (3½ oz) jamón, finely diced
½ teaspoon salt
60 g (2 oz/½ cup) grated mozzarella cheese
75 g (2½ oz/½ cup) plain (all-purpose) flour, extra, for dusting
1 egg, lightly beaten
120 g (4¼ oz/2 cups) panko crumbs
vegetable oil, for deep-frying
sea salt
Romesco sauce (page 274)

1 Melt the butter in a saucepan over low–medium heat, then add the onion and sauté for 2 minutes until soft and translucent. Add the flour and cook for 1 minute, stirring constantly to make sure there are no lumps.

2 Pour in the milk, a little at a time, making sure each addition of milk is incorporated into the flour before adding more. Continue to cook over low heat, stirring constantly and scraping the bottom of the pan to prevent the mixture from burning, until it thickens to the consistency of mashed potato.

3 Turn off the heat and transfer to a bowl. Mix in the jamón and salt. Cool slightly, then cover with plastic wrap and refrigerate overnight.

4 With floured hands, take 1 heaped spoonful of mixture and roll it into a ball. Poke your index finger into the centre of the ball to make a dent. Fill with some mozzarella cheese, pinch to seal the cheese inside, then roll it back into a ball. Repeat with the rest of the mixture.

5 Prepare 3 separate trays of flour, beaten egg and panko crumbs. Working in batches of 5 balls, place them in the tray with the flour, shake the tray and let them roll around until well coated. Repeat the process with the tray of beaten egg, and then finally roll the balls in the tray of panko crumbs. Use a fork to transfer the balls from tray to tray if necessary.

6 Pour the vegetable oil into a large saucepan until about one-third full, then heat the oil to 160°C (320°F) over medium heat. Use a kitchen thermometer to test if the oil is hot enough, or, alternatively, drop a cube of bread into the oil — it should turn golden brown within 30 seconds. It is important that the oil is at the correct temperature; if it is too hot, the croquettes will explode.

7 Deep-fry the croquettes in small batches for 2–3 minutes, or until golden brown. Drain on paper towel, sprinkle with sea salt and serve hot with the romesco sauce.

Zing BENEATH MY wings

SERVES 6-8

1.5 kg (3 lb 5 oz) chicken wings, cut at joints and discard wing tips
250 ml (8½ fl oz/1 cup) coconut milk
juice of ½ lemon
vegetable oil, for deep-frying
300 g (10½ oz/2 cups) plain (all-purpose) flour
1 tablespoon cayenne pepper
salt and pepper
a wedge of lime

NYONYA CURRY PASTE

1 tablespoon coriander seeds
1 teaspoon cumin seeds
1 teaspoon fennel seeds
2 cloves
80 g (3 oz) French shallots, peeled
2 large red chillies
1 cm (½ inch) piece fresh turmeric, peeled (or 1 teaspoon ground turmeric)
1 tablespoon sugar
½ teaspoon ground cinnamon
1 teaspoon freshly ground black pepper
2 teaspoons salt

1 To make the Nyonya curry paste, toast the coriander, cumin and fennel seeds and cloves in a dry frying pan over medium–low heat until fragrant, then use a mortar and pestle to grind them into a powder. Put the ground spices with the remaining curry paste ingredients into a food processor and blend everything together into a paste.

2 Put the chicken wings, coconut milk, lemon juice and curry paste into a large mixing bowl. Use your hands to massage the mixture into the chicken wings to make sure they are well coated. Cover with plastic wrap and place in the refrigerator to marinate for at least 1 hour, or ideally overnight.

3 Pour the vegetable oil into a medium saucepan until about one-third full, then heat the oil to 180°C (350°F) over medium–high heat. Test to see if the oil is hot enough by dipping a wooden chopstick in the oil — if the oil starts steadily bubbling around the chopstick, it's ready.

4 Combine the flour and cayenne pepper in a bowl, and season with salt and pepper. Dust the chicken pieces with the flour mixture, then shake off any excess and place on a tray.

5 Working in batches of 4 or 5 pieces, deep-fry the chicken wings for 5 minutes until golden. Drain on paper towel. Allow the temperature of the oil to come back up to 180°C (350°F), then deep-fry the chicken for a second time until golden brown and crispy. Drain on paper towel, then transfer to a serving plate. Squeeze some lime juice over the chicken before serving.

FORGET ABOUT THE 11 SECRET HERBS AND SPICES, THESE ZINGY FRIED CHICKEN WINGS WILL GIVE THAT GENTLEMAN WITH THE WHITE SUIT AND STRING TIE A RUN FOR HIS MONEY! THIS RECIPE IS A SPIN-OFF OF THE TRADITIONAL NYONYA FRIED CHICKEN CALLED 'INCHI KABIN'. IT IS AN EAST-MEETS-WEST DOUBLE HEAT COMBO OF NYONYA CURRY PASTE IN THE MARINADE AND CAYENNE PEPPER IN THE CRUNCHY COATING.

Five-spiced DUCK PANCAKES

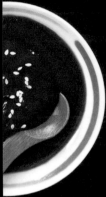

1.8 kg (4 lb) duck
2 teaspoons each Sichuan
  and black peppercorns
½ teaspoon ground white
  pepper
2 teaspoons five-spice
  powder
1 tablespoon salt
1 long strip of mandarin
  or orange peel
2 cm (¾ inch) piece ginger,
  peeled and thinly sliced
3 garlic cloves, peeled

3 star anise
olive oil
250 ml (8½ fl oz/1 cup)
  hoisin sauce
pinch of white sesame
  seeds, toasted
1 green cucumber,
  seeded and cut into
  5 cm (2 inch) lengths
3 spring onions
  (scallions), thinly sliced
  on the diagonal

PANCAKES (MAKES 20)
300 g (10½ oz/2 cups)
  plain (all-purpose)
  flour
pinch of salt
2 tablespoons caster
  (superfine) sugar
250 ml (8½ fl oz/1 cup)
  boiling water
sesame oil, to brush

1 To prepare the duck, first remove the neck, then clean the duck inside and out. Pat dry with paper towel. Separate the skin from the breast by running the index and middle fingers underneath the skin without tearing it. Use a chopstick for the hard-to-reach areas when necessary. Place the duck on a tray and refrigerate, uncovered, overnight to dry the skin.

2 To make the spice mix, use a mortar and pestle to grind the Sichuan and black peppercorns, white pepper, five-spice and salt to a powder.

3 Preheat the oven to 190°C (375°F). Rub 1 tablespoon of spice mix inside the duck cavity, then stuff it with mandarin peel, ginger, garlic and star anise. Bring the skin together to seal the cavity, then secure it with a bamboo skewer. Rub the remaining spice mix all over the duck skin, put the duck on a wire rack in a roasting tin, breast side up, and drizzle with olive oil. Place the duck in the oven and roast for 1½ hours, turning the tin around halfway through cooking time, for an even roasting on the skin. Keep the rendered duck fat in the roasting tin for another use (try the duck fat roast potatoes, pages 80–81).

4 Meanwhile, to make the pancakes, combine the flour, salt and sugar in a large bowl. Make a well in the centre and pour in the boiling water. Using a fork, draw in the flour until just combined. Turn the dough out onto a lightly floured surface and knead for 5 minutes, or until smooth. Wrap the dough in plastic wrap and set aside to rest for 20 minutes.

5 Roll the dough on a lightly floured surface into a log about 2.5 cm (1 inch) thick. Cut the log into 20 even pieces, then roll each portion into a ball. Flatten each ball in the palm of your hand to a 6 cm (2½ inch) round disc. Brush the top of one piece of flattened dough with sesame oil, place another piece on top and press lightly to join them together. Using a rolling pin, roll out the dough to a 15 cm (6 inch) pancake, about 2 mm (1/16 inch) thick. Repeat with the remaining dough balls. Stack the pancakes between sheets of baking paper.

6 To cook the pancakes, heat a large frying pan over low–medium heat (do not add any oil to the pan). Cook each pancake gently for 30 seconds on each side until it is puffed up slightly and starting to colour on a few spots. It should be cooked but still soft and malleable. Remove from the pan and, using your fingers (take care as the pancakes are hot), peel to separate the pancakes. Place the cooked pancakes on a plate and cover with a clean tea towel to keep them warm and prevent them from drying out. Repeat with the remaining pancakes.

7 Remove the skewer from the duck, then strain the liquid from the cavity through a fine sieve into a bowl. Discard the solids. Whisk 3 tablespoons of the strained liquid with the hoisin sauce to make a dipping sauce. Sprinkle the sesame seeds over the top.

8 Slice the skin off the duck into thin strips, then shred the duck meat into bite-sized pieces. Place the skin and meat on a platter with the cucumber strips and spring onions. To serve, smear a spoonful of hoisin sauce mixture on a pancake, top with duck meat and skin, garnish with cucumber strips and spring onions, then wrap it up like a crêpe.

I ORDER DUCK PANCAKES EVERY TIME I GO TO A CHINESE RESTAURANT. COOKING THE CRISPY PEKING DUCK IS A TEDIOUS SCIENCE PROJECT THAT INVOLVES DRYING THE DUCK WITH A FAN, THEN GLISTENING IT WITH MALTOSE BEFORE SHOWERING IT WITH LADLEFULS OF HOT OIL. THIS ALL SEEMS TOO DIFFICULT TO ATTEMPT AT HOME. HENCE, I OFFER THIS QUICK AND SIMPLE ALTERNATIVE OF BAKING THE DUCK IN THE OVEN WITH A GOOD RUB OF FIVE-SPICE FOR FLAVOUR.

MAKES
6*

*
MAKES 6
PARFAITS
IN 75 ML
(2½ FL OZ)
RAMEKINS

CHICKEN LIVER *parfait*

I HATED CHICKEN LIVER WITH A PASSION WHEN I WAS GROWING UP — AND MUM LOVED TO COOK IT FOR US! THE SMELL THAT LINGERED IN THE KITCHEN WAS ENOUGH TO PUT ME OFF, NOT TO MENTION THE OVERCOOKED METALLIC AFTERTASTE. MY PALATE HAS CHANGED A LOT OVER THE YEARS, AND SINCE DISCOVERING THE MAGICAL COMBO OF CHICKEN LIVER WITH CREAM, HERBS, SPICES AND BUTTER — LOTS OF BUTTER! — I AM NOW A CONVERTED MAN.

500 g (1 lb 2 oz) chicken livers
500 ml (17 fl oz/2 cups) full-cream milk
3 sprigs thyme
1 fresh bay leaf
200 g (7 oz) unsalted butter, plus 40 g (1½ oz) extra for cooking

2 tablespoons olive oil
1 French shallot, thinly sliced
1 garlic clove, finely chopped
25 ml (1 fl oz) whiskey, plus 1 tablespoon extra
100 ml (3½ fl oz) thickened (whipping) cream (35% fat)

1 teaspoon salt
freshly ground black pepper
1 loaf of brioche or sourdough baguette, thickly sliced
cranberry jam (or any fruit jam such as cherry, redcurrant or burnt fig)

1 Clean the chicken livers, trim off any sinews and cut into even pieces. Put the cleaned livers in a bowl with the milk, thyme and bay leaf, then place in the refrigerator to soak overnight, or for at least 6 hours.

2 Meanwhile, to clarify the butter, melt the butter gently in a saucepan over low–medium heat. The butter will separate into three layers: the impurities on top, clarified butter in the middle and milky solids at the bottom. Be careful that you don't overheat the butter or it will start bubbling and become cloudy. Skim off the impurities, then gently pour the clarified butter into a jug and set aside to cool. Discard the milky solids.

3 Strain the milk off the livers, but keep the thyme and bay leaf. Pat everything dry with paper towel.

4 Heat the olive oil in a large frying pan until the oil starts smoking. Working in batches so you don't overcrowd the pan, add the livers to the pan and seal for 30 seconds on each side. Remove and set aside. The livers should be firm but still pinkish inside.

5 Using the same pan, melt the extra butter, then add the shallot and garlic and sauté for 1 minute until soft and translucent. Return the livers to the pan with the thyme and bay leaf and stir to mix well.

6 Pour the whiskey into the pan, then carefully flambé the whiskey to burn off the alcohol. Tip everything except the clarified butter and cream into a food processor and let cool for a few minutes.

7 Process the cooked liver mixture until smooth. While the motor is still running, slowly pour in 150 ml (5 fl oz) of the clarified butter in a steady stream, then do the same with the cream. Blend for a further 2 minutes on high until it forms a smooth purée.

8 Push the purée through a fine sieve twice for a smooth consistency. Add the remaining tablespoon of whiskey to the parfait, season with the salt and pepper and mix well. Pour into ramekins and gently tap them on the kitchen bench to level the surface. Pour the remaining clarified butter over the top to a depth of 3 mm (⅛ inch), to make sure the parfait is completely sealed. Cover with plastic wrap and place in the refrigerator to set overnight. For best results, leave the parfait in the refrigerator for 5 days or so, to allow the flavours to develop.

9 Serve the parfait with thick slices of brioche lightly toasted on a chargrill pan, with the cranberry jam.

GUINNESS *battered* PRAWNS

SERVES 4

NO MATTER IF IT'S DEEP-FRIED BATTERED FISH, VEGETABLES OR EVEN A MARS BAR, THE SECRET TO A LIGHT AND CRUNCHY BATTER IS BEER. I PREFER TO USE A FULL-BODIED STOUT LIKE GUINNESS; IT HAS A HINT OF SPICY WORCESTERSHIRE SAUCE AROMAS, SUBTLE COFFEE-TOFFEE FLAVOURS AND A CHOCOLATEY FINISH. THESE GUINNESS-BATTERED PRAWNS ARE ALWAYS A HIT AT PARTIES — THEY'LL DISAPPEAR JUST AS QUICKLY AS YOU TAKE THEM OUT OF THE HOT OIL!

225 g (8 oz/1½ cups) plain (all-purpose) flour
2 teaspoons baking powder
1 teaspoon salt
pinch of ground black pepper
330 ml (11 oz) bottle Guinness Draught beer
vegetable oil, for deep-frying
500 g (1 lb 2 oz) raw prawns (shrimp), peeled and deveined
pinch of cayenne pepper
Wasabi mayo (page 270)

1 Sift the flour, baking powder, salt and pepper into a large mixing bowl. Gradually pour in the Guinness and whisk everything together until well combined; it should be a light and frothy batter with no lumps. Place in the refrigerator to rest for at least 20 minutes.

2 Pour the vegetable oil into a medium saucepan until about half full, then heat the oil to 190°C (375°F) over medium–high heat. Test to see if the oil is hot enough by dipping a wooden chopstick into the hot oil — if the oil starts steadily bubbling around the chopstick, it's ready. Working in batches, dip the prawns in the batter, then carefully drop them into the hot oil and deep-fry for 1 minute, or until golden brown. Remove and drain on paper towel. Sprinkle with cayenne pepper and serve with wasabi mayo.

Pandan CHICKEN

500 g (1 lb 2 oz) boneless,
  skinless chicken breasts,
  cut into 5 × 2 cm (2 × ¾ inch)
  strips
about 15 pandan (screw pine)
  leaves (see note page 93)
about 30 bamboo skewers
500 ml (17 fl oz/2 cups)
  vegetable oil

MARINADE
2 tablespoons curry powder
1 tablespoon ground
  turmeric
3 tablespoons coconut cream
2 lemongrass stalks, white
  part only, finely chopped
3 garlic cloves, finely
  chopped

1 tablespoon fish sauce
1 teaspoon sugar
pinch each of salt and
  ground white pepper

1 Combine the marinade ingredients in a large mixing
bowl, add the chicken strips and rub the marinade
into the chicken until well coated. Cover with plastic
wrap and place in the refrigerator to marinate for at least
1 hour, or preferably overnight.

2 Cut the pandan leaves into 10 cm (4 inch) lengths,
then gather the leaves up into one bunch and gently
twist the bunch to bruise the leaves; this will help to
release the essence. Be careful not to tear the leaves.

3 Place a piece of chicken at one end of a pandan leaf.
Fold the leaf over, then roll up until the whole leaf is
wrapped around the chicken. Insert a skewer through
the centre of the parcel to secure the leaf and chicken
together. Repeat the process with all the chicken strips.

4 Heat the vegetable oil in a frying pan over medium–
high heat. Fry the pandan chicken in batches for
2–3 minutes, or until the chicken is cooked. Remove
and drain on paper towel. Serve hot; unwrap to eat and
discard the pandan leaves.

MAKES
25
TO
30

THIS IS SUPER SIMPLE AND FAST TO MAKE, BUT YOU DO NEED TO FIND SOME
PANDAN LEAVES AT YOUR LOCAL ASIAN GREENGROCER BEFORE YOU START.
THE PANDAN LEAVES GIVE THE CHICKEN A SUBTLE SWEETNESS AND AROMA,
AND ALSO HELP TO KEEP THE MEAT MOIST WHILE IT COOKS.

Oysters WITH CUCUMBER SORBET & pepper spray

1 dozen oysters, freshly
    shucked
crushed ice, for serving
20 g (¾ oz) salmon roe

CUCUMBER SORBET
1 tablespoon sugar
1 tablespoon glucose
125 ml (4 fl oz/½ cup) water
2 Lebanese (short)
    cucumbers, peeled
juice of 1 lime
3 tablespoons vodka

PEPPER SPRAY
1 tablespoon Tabasco sauce
1 teaspoon white vinegar
juice of ½ lemon
pinch of salt
4 × 5 ml (⅛ fl oz) atomisers
    (see note)

1 To make the cucumber sorbet, put the sugar, glucose and water into a small saucepan and bring to the boil over medium heat, stirring until the sugar has dissolved. Once boiling, remove the sugar syrup from the heat and let it cool completely before transferring to the refrigerator to chill.

2 Purée the whole cucumbers in a small food processor or blender, then add the lime juice, vodka and cold sugar syrup. Stir well, then strain through a fine sieve. Churn the mixture in an ice cream maker according to the manufacturer's directions. Alternatively, pour the mixture into a baking tin and let it set in the freezer. Scrape the frozen cucumber ice block into powdered snow just before serving.

3 To make the pepper spray, mix all the ingredients together and then pour into the atomisers.

4 To serve, place the oysters on some crushed ice. Top each oyster with a teaspoon of cucumber sorbet, then garnish with ½ teaspoon of salmon roe. Invite guests to pepper spray the oysters as much or as little as they like using the atomisers.

Note: You can find small atomisers at bargain shops, cosmetic stores or pharmacies. Sterilise the bottles with boiling water before using them.

THIS IS A FUN RECIPE FOR
THOSE WHO ARE SCEPTICAL
ABOUT OYSTERS. I THINK
THE FLAVOUR COMBO OF
OYSTER AND CUCUMBER
IS A MARRIAGE MADE IN
HEAVEN. THE CUCUMBER
SORBET KEEPS THE
OYSTERS CHILLED, AND
ITS SWEETNESS PROVIDES
A WONDERFUL CONTRAST
TO THE BRININESS OF THE
OYSTERS. THEN THE FUN
PART: SPRAYING YOUR
FOOD WITH TINY BOTTLES
OF PEPPER SPRAY IS
GUARANTEED TO BRING OUT
YOUR INNER CHILD.

Grilled TUNA JAW with TERIYAKI glaze

2 × 500 g (1 lb 2 oz) fresh tuna jaws (see note)

250 ml (8½ fl oz/1 cup) teriyaki sauce

3 tablespoons light soy sauce

125 ml (4 fl oz/½ cup) mirin

1 teaspoon sesame oil

3 garlic cloves, crushed

5 cm (2 inch) piece ginger, grated

1 lemon, halved

DIPPING SAUCE

1 tablespoon grated daikon (white radish)

2 tablespoons light soy sauce

1 tablespoon mirin

1 teaspoon sesame oil

1 Wash the tuna jaws, remove any traces of blood and then pat dry with paper towel.

2 Put the teriyaki sauce, soy sauce, mirin, sesame oil, garlic and ginger in a large mixing bowl. Rub the mixture into the tuna jaws, then cover and place in the refrigerator to marinate for 1 hour. Meanwhile, combine the ingredients for the dipping sauce.

3 Heat up the barbecue grill to medium. Place the tuna jaws on the barbecue, close the lid, and cook for 8–10 minutes on each side, basting the jaws with the marinade from time to time. Transfer to a serving platter and squeeze over some lemon juice. Serve with the dipping sauce.

Note: *Tuna jaw is part of the offcut of a whole tuna head left after filleting. The tuna heads are hard to come by, but try your luck at your local fish markets; sometimes they might have a few tuna heads in the cool room and will let you have them. A word of warning though: the tuna head is massive and you do need to know how to break it down to save the jaws only. One tuna head will give you two tuna jaws.*

SERVES
4

I STUMBLED ACROSS A MASSIVE TUNA HEAD IN A STYROFOAM
BOX AT THE FISH MARKET, READY TO BE THROWN OUT. I ASKED
THE FISHMONGER WHETHER I COULD BUY THE JAWS TO USE FOR
MY COOKING. HE LOOKED AT ME STRANGELY AND SAID, 'TAKE
THE WHOLE THING!' NEXT THING I KNEW, I WAS DRIVING
HOME WITH A TUNA HEAD ON THE PASSENGER SEAT.

TUNA JAW IS ONE OF THE SWEETEST AND MOST TENDER
PARTS OF THE FISH, SO IT IS WELL WORTH THE EFFORT
TO HUNT ONE DOWN FOR THIS RECIPE. YOU'LL BE
SURPRISED HOW MUCH MEAT YOU GET FROM
ONE JAW.

Otak-otak PANGGANG

THIS IS A POPULAR CLASSIC NYONYA SNACK THAT YOU CAN FIND ALMOST EVERYWHERE IN MALAYSIA. THE FISH PASTE IS WRAPPED IN BANANA LEAF PARCELS AND THEN EITHER STEAMED OR GRILLED ON A BARBECUE. I PREFER THE LATTER VERSION AS IT HAS A NICE, SMOKY FLAVOUR.

OTAK-OTAK ACTUALLY MEANS 'BRAINS' IN MALAY, BECAUSE THE COOKED FISH PASTE IS SOFT AND ALMOST SQUISHY, LIKE A BRAIN! BUT DON'T WORRY, YOU WON'T TURN INTO A ZOMBIE ANYTIME SOON. 'BRAINZZZ ...'

{GRILLED SPICY FISH PASTE IN BANANA LEAF}

250 ml (8½ fl oz/1 cup) Rempah spice paste (page 272)

125 ml (4 fl oz/½ cup) coconut cream

4 kaffir lime leaves, very thinly sliced (see note)

1 tablespoon sugar

1 teaspoon salt

2 large banana leaves, cut into 20 cm (8 inch) squares, cleaned (you will need 12–15 squares)

a handful of toothpicks

FISH PASTE

500 g (1 lb 2 oz) snapper fillets (or use any firm white fish such as barramundi, cod or ling)

1 tablespoon cornflour (cornstarch)

pinch of salt

½ teaspoon ground white pepper

125 ml (4 fl oz/½ cup) iced water

Note: To cut kaffir lime leaves into long thin strips, stack the leaves together, roll them tightly then very thinly slice. This cooking technique is called 'chiffonade'.

1 To make the fish paste, put 300 g (10½ oz) of the fish fillets in a food processor, then add the cornflour, salt and white pepper and blend into a paste. With the processor still running, pour the iced water into the mixture in a steady stream, and blend until it forms a sticky paste.

2 With cleaned hands, collect the fish paste in one hand and throw it against the side of a mixing bowl. Do this 8–10 times until the fish paste becomes sticky and elastic. This technique gives the paste a nice springy texture when cooked. Chop up the remaining 200 g (7 oz) of the fish fillets into 1 cm (½ inch) cubes and mix into the fish paste.

3 Scoop out 30 g (1 oz) of the fish paste and put it into another mixing bowl. Add the rempah spice paste, coconut cream and kaffir lime leaves, then season with the sugar and salt. Stir well and set aside.

4 Scald the banana leaves with hot water to soften them, then pat dry. Alternatively, place the leaves in a microwave for 30 seconds or fan the leaves over a naked flame on a gas stove.

5 To assemble, spread a teaspoon of the spice paste in the middle of the banana leaf, put a tablespoon of fish paste on top, then cover with another teaspoon of spice paste over the top. Gently fold the leaf over the mixture and secure both ends with toothpicks. Repeat until all the fish paste is used.

6 Heat up a barbecue and grill the fish parcels for 5 minutes on each side. Pile the banana leaf parcels onto a serving platter.

MAKES

12

TO

15

Chorizo & PRAWN SKEWERS

SERVES 4

* ALLOW 3 OR 4 PRAWNS PER PERSON

GARLIC PRAWNS AND CHORIZO ARE TWO OF MY FAVOURITE SPANISH TAPAS SNACKS. I LIKE TO CALL THIS COMBINATION 'SURF-AND-TURF ON A STICK' — IT'S A MATCH MADE IN HEAVEN! THESE ARE A PERFECT SUMMERTIME NIBBLE, WASHED DOWN WITH SOME COLD BEER. THROW ANOTHER PRAWN ON THE BARBIE, LOVE!

20–25 small bamboo skewers
500 g (1 lb 2 oz) raw prawns (shrimp), peeled and deveined, tails left on
3 garlic cloves, roughly chopped
1 red chilli, roughly chopped

1 lemongrass stalk, white part only, roughly chopped
2 tablespoons olive oil
2 chorizo sausages, cut into 1 cm ($\frac{1}{2}$ inch) thick slices
a few lemon wedges

1 Soak the bamboo skewers in water for 10 minutes. Combine the prawns, garlic, chilli, lemongrass and olive oil in a bowl, then cover and place in the refrigerator to marinate for at least 30 minutes.

2 Wrap a prawn around a slice of chorizo, then insert a skewer through the prawn and chorizo to secure them together. Repeat with the rest of the prawns.

3 Preheat a barbecue hotplate or frying pan and cook the prawns for 1 minute on both sides, or until the prawns are cooked. Squeeze over some lemon juice before serving.

on the
SIDE

BUDDHA'S DELIGHT ❖ Deep-fried salt & pepper tofu ❖ ASIAN GREENS — CHOY SUM; BELACHAN KANGKONG; GAI LAN; GAI CHOY WITH NAM YU; BABY BOK CHOY ❖ Baby tomatoes & bambini bocconcini ❖ Acar awak (spicy pickled vegetables) ❖ BRUSSELS SPROUTS, SPECK & HAZELNUTS WITH MUSTARD DRESSING ❖ Watermelon, baby tomato, chèvre & candied walnut salad ❖ ROAST SPICED CAULIFLOWER & CORN SALAD ❖ Roast potatoes, black pudding & pork belly

THERE IS AN OLD CHINESE SAYING THAT A COMPLETE MEAL SHOULD CONSIST OF 'THREE DISHES, ONE SOUP', WITH A BOWL OF STEAMED RICE. ONCE YOU'VE CHOSEN YOUR MAIN DISH, CHOOSE ONE OR TWO SIDE DISHES TO GO WITH IT; THEY DON'T HAVE TO BE FANCY — KEEP IT SIMPLE WITH A BALANCE OF FLAVOURS THAT COMPLEMENT ONE OTHER.

bean curd sheets

Chinese cabbage

dried lily buds (golden needles)

bamboo shoots

glass noodles

cloud ear (black) fungus

BUDDHA'S delight

NOT MANY PEOPLE CAN SAY THAT THEY HAVE COOKED FOR THE DALAI LAMA, BUT I AM EXTREMELY HONOURED AND HUMBLED TO HAVE HAD THAT OPPORTUNITY WHEN I COOKED THIS DISH FOR HIS HOLINESS DURING MY TIME ON 'MASTERCHEF'.

BUDDHA'S DELIGHT, ALSO KNOWN AS 'LUO HAN ZHAI', IS A VEGETARIAN DISH TRADITIONALLY ENJOYED BY BUDDHIST MONKS. THIS POPULAR DISH HAS BEEN PASSED THROUGH GENERATIONS AND, MUCH LIKE CHINESE WHISPERS, THIS HAS RESULTED IN MANY VARIATIONS, INCLUDING A NON-VEGETARIAN VERSION THAT IS COOKED IN OYSTER SAUCE WITH THE ADDITION OF SEAFOOD. DON'T LET THE LIST OF INGREDIENTS IN THIS RECIPE FREAK YOU OUT! IT MAY LOOK DAUNTING, BUT THIS DISH IS VERY SIMPLE TO MAKE AND IS A ONE-POT WONDER.

enoki mushrooms

red dates (jujubes)

nam yu (red fermented tofu)

baby corn

carrots

dried shiitake mushrooms

see recipe over →

BUDDHA'S *delight*

DRIED INGREDIENTS
50 g (2 oz) packet glass noodles
15–20 dried lily buds (golden needles)
5 dried shiitake mushrooms
1 large cloud ear (black) fungus
1 bunch fatt choy (black moss)
10 red dates (jujubes)

FRESH INGREDIENTS
1 carrot, thinly sliced
50 g (2 oz) bamboo shoots, thinly sliced
5 baby corn
10 snow peas (mangetouts)
50 g (2 oz) bunch enoki mushrooms,
  ends trimmed
200 g (7 oz) Chinese cabbage, washed
  and cut into 3 cm (1¼ inch) strips

4 tablespoons vegetable oil
3 garlic cloves, finely chopped
2 French shallots, thinly sliced
2 cubes nam yu (red fermented tofu),
  mashed (optional)
250 ml (8½ fl oz/1 cup) water
3 tablespoons light soy sauce
2 tablespoons Shaoxing rice wine
1 teaspoon sesame oil
1 tablespoon cornflour (cornstarch),
  mixed with 4 tablespoons water
2 oiled bean curd sheets, cut into 30 cm
  (12 inch) squares

1 Prepare all the dried ingredients first. Soak the glass noodles in a bowl of water for 1 hour until softened, then drain. Soak the lily buds in hot water for 30 minutes until softened, then trim off any hard stalks and tie each bud into a knot. Soak the shiitake mushrooms in hot water for 1 hour, then drain. Remove and discard the mushroom stalks, then slice the mushrooms in half. Soak the cloud ear fungus in lukewarm water for 30 minutes, then tear into smaller pieces. Soak the fatt choy in water for 30 minutes until softened. Soak the red dates in water for 30 minutes, then halve them and remove the seeds.

2 Prepare all the fresh ingredients as directed and set aside.

3 Heat the vegetable oil in a wok over medium–high heat and fry the garlic and shallots for 2 minutes until fragrant. Add the mashed nam yu cubes and cook, stirring, for another minute.

4 Add the shiitake mushrooms, carrot, bamboo shoots, baby corn and snow peas. Stir-fry for 2 minutes, then add the lily buds, red dates, cloud ear fungus and enoki mushrooms, and stir-fry for another 2 minutes. Lastly, add the Chinese cabbage and give it a quick stir.

5 Add the water, soy sauce, rice wine and sesame oil, and simmer for 5 minutes until the vegetables are tender, stirring occasionally.

6 Stir in the glass noodles, then add the fatt choy but try to keep it in one clump by not stirring it too much. Thicken the sauce by adding the cornflour and water mixture, then let it braise for few minutes.

7 Just before the vegetables are ready, lay the bean curd sheets in a large bowl or round claypot, with the corners hanging over the rim of the bowl. Pick the fatt choy out of the wok and place it in the bowl, on top of the bean curd sheet, then fill with the vegetables. Pick up the corners of the bean curd sheets and fold them over to enclose the vegetables.

8 Place an upside-down serving plate over the bowl, then carefully pick up both the plate and bowl and flip it over. Use chopsticks to tear the bean curd parcel apart, revealing the vegetables inside.

SERVES
6-8

I CAN UNDERSTAND WHY MANY PEOPLE THINK TOFU IS BLAND AND BORING. BUT IT IS ACTUALLY EXTREMELY VERSATILE AND LENDS ITSELF WELL TO A VARIETY OF FLAVOURS AND COOKING TECHNIQUES. I PREFER SOFT SILKEN TOFU, BUT IT NEEDS TO BE HANDLED WITH CARE AS IT IS VERY DELICATE AND CRUMBLES EASILY. THIS RECIPE IS ALL ABOUT TEXTURES — THE SOFT, SILKY SMOOTH TOFU ON THE INSIDE AND THE SALTY AND PEPPERY CRISPY COATING ON THE OUTSIDE. I GUARANTEE YOU'LL NEVER LOOK AT TOFU THE SAME WAY AGAIN.

Deep-fried SALT & PEPPER tofu

1 teaspoon salt

1 teaspoon caster (superfine) sugar

½ teaspoon ground white pepper

½ teaspoon five-spice powder

vegetable oil, for deep-frying, plus 2 tablespoons extra

125 g (4 oz/1 cup) cornflour (cornstarch)

1 block (300 g/10½ oz) silken firm tofu, cut into 6 pieces

2 garlic cloves, finely chopped

1 bird's eye chilli, seeded and thinly sliced

1 spring onion (scallion), green part only, chopped

1 Combine the salt, sugar, white pepper and five-spice together in a bowl, then set aside.

2 Pour the vegetable oil into a medium saucepan until about one-third full, then heat the oil to 180°C (350°F) over medium–high heat. Test to see if the oil is hot enough by dipping a wooden chopstick in the oil — if the oil starts steadily bubbling around the chopstick, it's ready.

3 Put the cornflour in a bowl and add the tofu. Gently turn the tofu to coat in the cornflour, then shake off any excess flour. Deep-fry the tofu for 2 minutes, or until golden brown. Drain on paper towel.

4 Heat the extra 2 tablespoons vegetable oil in a wok over high heat, then add the garlic, chilli and spring onion and stir-fry for 1 minute until fragrant.

5 While the tofu pieces are still hot, place them in a large metal bowl with 1 teaspoon of the salt and pepper mixture, and toss them in the mixture until nicely coated. Transfer the tofu to a serving plate, then sprinkle with the fried garlic and chilli, and serve the remaining salt and pepper mixture on the side.

Asian greens

A HUGE VARIETY OF ASIAN VEGETABLES ARE AVAILABLE IN THE
SUPERMARKET THESE DAYS. THEY ARE EASY TO COOK, HEALTHY AND
FULL OF FLAVOUR, AND I THINK THEY ARE TOTALLY UNDERRATED;
MANY PEOPLE SHY AWAY FROM THEM SIMPLY BECAUSE THEY DON'T
KNOW WHAT TO DO WITH THEM. KEEP IT SIMPLE IS THE KEY — LESS
IS MORE. ALL YOU NEED IS A WOK AND A FEW INGREDIENTS, AND THE
VEGETABLES ONLY NEED A QUICK STIR-FRY, SO THEY STAY CRUNCHY
AND RETAIN ALL THEIR NUTRIENTS.

THE ASIAN GREENS USED IN THESE FIVE RECIPES ARE ALL
INTERCHANGEABLE, SO MIX AND MATCH HOWEVER YOU LIKE. THAT'S
THE BEAUTY OF COOKING ASIAN GREENS: YOU CAN'T GO WRONG.
WASH THE VEGETABLES WELL BEFORE COOKING. A GOOD TIP IS TO
SOAK THEM IN A SINK FILLED WITH TAP WATER, WITH A TABLESPOON
OF SALT. ANY DIRT OR SOIL WILL GET WASHED OUT AND FALL TO THE
BOTTOM OF THE SINK, AND THE SALT WILL KILL ANY SLUGS OR BUGS
HIDDEN IN THE LEAVES.

SERVES

4

CHOY SUM

CHOY SUM LITERALLY MEANS THE 'VEGETABLE HEART'
IN CANTONESE. IT HAS BROAD, DARK GREEN LEAVES,
WITH SOFT GREEN STEMS, SOMETIMES WITH
YELLOW FLOWERS. CHOY SUM CAN BE EASILY
OVERCOOKED AND ONLY NEEDS A MINUTE OR
TWO IN THE WOK. I HAVE USED FISH CAKE
TO GO WITH THE CHOY SUM IN THIS RECIPE,
BUT YOU COULD ALSO USE FISH BALLS, LAP
CHEONG (CHINESE SAUSAGES; SEE NOTE
PAGE 94) OR FIRM TOFU CUBES.

4 tablespoons vegetable oil
3 garlic cloves, finely chopped
2 French shallots, thinly
*   sliced*
10 g ($\frac{1}{2}$ oz) fish cake, thinly
*   sliced (see note)*
1 bunch choy sum, ends
*   trimmed, washed and cut*
*   into 5 cm (2 inch) lengths*

2 tablespoons light soy sauce,
*   plus extra to serve*
dash of sesame oil
2 tablespoons oyster sauce

1 Heat the vegetable oil in a wok, add the garlic and shallots and fry
until golden. Remove from the wok and set aside (keeping the oil
in the wok).

2 Reheat the wok, then add the fish cake slices and stir-fry for
about 1 minute, or until lightly brown on the edges. Add the choy
sum and stir-fry for 30 seconds. Add the soy sauce and sesame oil,
toss to combine, then stir-fry for a further 30 seconds.

3 Transfer to a serving plate and sprinkle the fried garlic and
shallots over the top. Give it another splash of soy sauce and
drizzle the oyster sauce all over.

*Note: Fish cake can be found in Asian grocers or major supermarkets. It comes in a long,
thin block in a sealed packet.*

61 • ON THE SIDE

BELACHAN kangkong

IN CHINESE WE CALL THIS DISH 'THE SCENERY OF MALAYA', AND IT'S EASY TO SEE WHY. THE LUSCIOUS VIVID GREEN OF THE KANGKONG, THE INTOXICATING SMELL OF BELACHAN SHRIMP PASTE AND THE HOT, FIERY CHILLI FLAVOUR WILL IMMEDIATELY TRANSPORT YOU TO A MALAYSIAN GRANDMA'S KITCHEN IN A RURAL VILLAGE SOMEWHERE IN THE TROPICAL RAINFOREST.

10 g ($\frac{1}{2}$ oz) belachan (dried shrimp paste)

3 garlic cloves, peeled

2 French shallots, peeled

1 large red chilli, whole, plus 1 extra, sliced diagonally

2 tablespoons dried shrimp, soaked in hot water for 10 minutes and drained

4 tablespoons vegetable oil

1 bunch kangkong (water spinach), stalks trimmed, washed and cut into 5 cm (2 inch) lengths

2 tablespoons light soy sauce

1 Wrap the belachan in foil and toast in a frying pan for 2 minutes on each side. Remove from the pan and cool before removing the foil.

2 Put the garlic, shallots, whole chilli, dried shrimp and belachan in a food processor and whiz to form a rough paste.

3 Heat the vegetable oil in a wok, then add the spice paste and fry until fragrant. Add the kangkong and stir-fry for 30 seconds. Add the soy sauce and toss everything together, then add the sliced chilli and stir-fry for a further 30 seconds. Transfer to a serving plate.

SERVES
4

GAI LAN

GAI LAN IS ONE OF MY FAVOURITE ASIAN VEGETABLES, AND IT IS A VERY POPULAR YUM CHA DISH IN CHINESE RESTAURANTS. SIMILAR TO KALE OR BROCCOLI, GAI LAN (OR CHINESE BROCCOLI AS IT IS ALSO CALLED) HAS CRISP, THICK STEMS AND DARK GREEN LEAVES. IT DOES TAKE A LITTLE LONGER TO COOK COMPARED TO THE OTHER ASIAN VEGETABLES — ABOUT 2 TO 3 MINUTES.

4 tablespoons vegetable oil
3 garlic cloves plus 2 garlic cloves, all finely chopped
1 bunch gai lan (Chinese broccoli), washed and cut into 5 cm (2 inch) lengths

2 tablespoons light soy sauce, plus extra to serve
dash of sesame oil
pinch of ground white pepper

1 Heat the vegetable oil in a wok, add 3 cloves chopped garlic and fry until golden. Remove from the wok and set aside (keeping the oil in the wok).

2 Reheat the wok, then add the remaining garlic and the gai lan and stir-fry for 30 seconds. Add the soy sauce and sesame oil, toss to combine, cover with the lid and let it steam for 2 minutes.

3 Stir well and transfer to a serving plate. Sprinkle the fried garlic over the top, then give it another dash of soy sauce and a smidgen of white pepper.

SERVES
4

Gai choy with NAM YU

GAI CHOY — ALSO KNOWN AS CHINESE MUSTARD GREENS OR MUSTARD
CABBAGE — IS NOT EVERYONE'S CUP OF TEA, AS IT CAN BE VERY PEPPERY
AND TENDS TO LOOK A BIT SAD AND DULL GREEN ONCE COOKED. BUT IT
IS EXTREMELY NUTRITIOUS AND ONE CUPFUL CAN PROVIDE THE ENTIRE
RECOMMENDED DAILY REQUIREMENT OF VITAMIN C.

SURPRISINGLY THE MUSTARDY TASTE OF THE GAI CHOY GOES REALLY WELL
WITH OTHER STRONGLY FLAVOURED INGREDIENTS, SUCH AS THE SALTY
FERMENTED NAM YU USED IN THIS RECIPE.

4 tablespoons vegetable oil
2 garlic cloves, finely chopped
*4 bunches gai choy (Chinese
    mustard greens), stalks
    trimmed, separated and
    washed*
2 tablespoons light soy sauce
*3 cubes nam yu (red fermented
    tofu), plus 1 extra cube*

1 Heat the vegetable oil in a wok, add the
garlic and fry until golden, then add the
gai choy and stir-fry for 1 further minute.
Add the soy sauce and nam yu cubes and use
a spatula to squash the nam yu into crumbs.
Toss to combine well, then stir-fry for a
further 30 seconds.

2 Transfer the gai choy to a serving plate.
Crumble the extra cube of nam yu and
sprinkle it over the top.

SERVES
4

Baby bok choy

I LIKE BABY BOK CHOY BETTER THAN THE FULLY GROWN VERSION, WHICH CAN BE TOUGH AND NOT AS SWEET. THIS VERSATILE VEGETABLE CAN BE SERVED AS A SIMPLE STIR-FRY, LIKE THIS RECIPE, TO GO WITH A BOWL OF STEAMED RICE OR AS AN ACCOMPANIMENT TO MANY CHINESE NOODLE DISHES.

4 tablespoons vegetable oil
2 garlic cloves, finely chopped
2 lap cheong (Chinese sausages, see note page 94), thinly sliced on the diagonal
4 bunches baby bok choy, stalks trimmed, leaves separated and washed
2 tablespoons light soy sauce, plus extra to serve
2 tablespoons Shaoxing rice wine

1 Heat the vegetable oil in a wok over medium–high heat, then add the garlic and lap cheong and fry until the sausage is crispy. Add the bok choy and stir-fry for 30 seconds, then add the soy sauce and rice wine. Toss to combine, then stir-fry for a further 30 seconds. Transfer to a serving plate and give the bok choy another splash of soy sauce.

Baby TOMATOES & bambini BOCCONCINI

WHAT MAKES THIS DISH SO SPECIAL AND BEAUTIFUL IS THE QUALITY OF THE PRODUCE. USUALLY I AM NOT THE KIND OF PERSON WHO WILL GO AND SPLURGE ON SOME FANCY, EXPENSIVE INGREDIENT, BUT WHEN IT COMES TO TOMATOES, IT IS WELL WORTHWHILE SPENDING A LITTLE BIT MORE TO GET THE BEST TOMATOES IN THE MARKET. THIS DISH IS ALL ABOUT THE UMAMI FLAVOUR OF THE BABY TOMATOES, SO TRY TO FIND A VARIETY SUCH AS PERINO, ROMA, HEIRLOOM OR KUMATO, WHICH WILL GIVE YOU A SWEETER, RICHER AND ALMOST MEATY FLAVOUR. THEN ALSO TRY TO GET THE SOFTEST, CREAMIEST BAMBINI BOCCONCINI AND THE BEST EXTRA-VIRGIN OLIVE OIL YOU CAN FIND.

1 × 400 g (14 oz) punnet baby (roma) tomatoes, halved

10–15 bambini bocconcini, halved

1 tablespoon candied (caramelised) balsamic vinegar

2 tablespoons extra-virgin olive oil

sea salt flakes

freshly ground black pepper

1 Put the tomatoes and bocconcini in a large mixing bowl. Drizzle with the balsamic vinegar and olive oil, and season well with salt and pepper. Toss to combine well, then transfer to a serving plate.

acar AWAK

SERVES **4*** <u></u> *GENEROUSLY* *

{SPICY PICKLED VEGETABLES}

1 litre (34 fl oz/4 cups) water

250 ml (8½ fl oz/1 cup) white vinegar

2 tablespoons salt

2 tablespoons sugar

100 g (3½ oz) carrot, cut into 5 cm (2 inch) long strips

100 g (3½ oz) snake (long) beans, cut into 5 cm (2 inch) lengths

100 g (3½ oz) cauliflower, separated into small florets

100 g (3½ oz) eggplant (aubergine), cut into 5 cm (2 inch) long strips (optional)

300 g (10½ oz) cabbage, cut into 2 cm (¾ inch) wide, 5 cm (2 inch) long strips

100 g (3½ oz) pineapple, cut into small pieces

PICKLED CUCUMBER

250 g (9 oz) green or Lebanese (short) cucumber

1 tablespoon salt

5 tablespoons sugar

3 tablespoons white vinegar

SPICE PASTE

125 ml (4 fl oz/½ cup) vegetable oil

300 ml (10 fl oz) Rempah spice paste (page 272)

2 tablespoons tamarind purée, mixed with 2 tablespoons water (see note)

110 g (3¾ oz/½ cup) sugar

1 tablespoon salt

100 g (3½ oz/⅔ cup) peanuts, toasted and roughly chopped

1 tablespoon sesame seeds, toasted

NEARLY EVERY COUNTRY AROUND THE WORLD HAS THEIR VERSION OF PICKLED VEGETABLES. GERMANS HAVE SAUERKRAUT, KOREANS HAVE KIM CHI, ITALIANS HAVE GIARDINIERA AND MALAYSIANS HAVE ACAR AWAK. THIS IS A CLASSIC PERANAKAN PICKLED VEGETABLE RELISH; IT HAS A SPICY, SWEET AND SOUR TASTE THAT GOES REALLY WELL WITH MEAT DISHES. I REMEMBER AS A CHILD IN MALAYSIA WHEN MY MUM USED TO MAKE THESE SPICY PICKLED VEGETABLES BY THE BUCKET LOAD. SHE THEN PORTIONED THEM INTO SMALLER PLASTIC CONTAINERS AND GAVE THEM TO THE NEIGHBOURS.

ACAR AWAK KEEPS VERY WELL IN AN AIRTIGHT CONTAINER IN THE REFRIGERATOR FOR UP TO A FEW MONTHS, AND THE FLAVOUR INTENSIFIES OVER TIME.

1 To make the pickled cucumber, cut the cucumber lengthwise into quarters (without peeling). Use a spoon to scrape out the seeds, then cut into 5 cm (2 inch) long strips. Put the cucumber, salt, sugar and vinegar into a bowl, mix well, and set aside for an hour to pickle. Then squeeze out as much liquid from the cucumber as you can, and lay the strips on a tray lined with paper towel.

2 Put the water, vinegar, salt and sugar in a large saucepan and bring to the boil. Blanch the carrot, snake beans and cauliflower for 1 minute, then add the eggplant (if using) and cabbage and blanch for another minute. Drain the vegetables in a colander.

3 To make the spice paste, heat the vegetable oil in a wok over medium–high heat and fry the rempah paste for 5 minutes until fragrant and dark brown in colour. Season with the tamarind purée, sugar and salt, and cook for another 5 minutes until the spice paste thickens. Mix well, then turn off the heat and leave to cool completely.

4 Add the blanched vegetables, pickled cucumber and pineapple to the wok, and stir well to coat in the spicy paste. Transfer to a serving dish and sprinkle with chopped peanuts and toasted sesame seeds.

Note: Tamarind purée is a concentrated paste sold in a jar and found in Asian food stores and major supermarkets. If you can only find fresh tamarind pulp, then you can make the tamarind water by mixing 1 heaped tablespoon of tamarind pulp (this is found in blocks or cakes that still contain the seeds) with 3 tablespoons of warm water. Press through a sieve to extract the pulp.

BRUSSELS SPROUTS, *speck* & *hazelnuts*
WITH MUSTARD DRESSING

2 tablespoons olive oil
500 g (1 lb 2 oz) brussels sprouts, halved
150 g (5 oz) speck (or use bacon), cut into strips
50 g (2 oz/$\frac{1}{3}$ cup) hazelnuts, toasted

DRESSING
1 teaspoon hot English mustard
1 tablespoon balsamic vinegar
2 tablespoons extra-virgin olive oil
pinch of salt and pepper

1 Preheat the oven to 220°C (430°F). Heat the olive oil in a frying pan over medium-high heat and fry the brussels sprouts, cut side down, in batches for 1 minute, or until charred, then transfer to a baking dish.

2 In the same pan, fry the speck until crispy on the edges, then mix together with the brussels sprouts. Place the dish in the oven and cook for 20 minutes, or until the brussels sprouts are nicely charred and crispy on the outside. Meanwhile, mix all the dressing ingredients together and set aside.

3 Transfer the brussels sprouts to a serving plate and toss together with the hazelnuts, then drizzle over the dressing.

BADLY PREPARED BRUSSELS SPROUTS CAN BE HARD TO SWALLOW. I'VE SEEN SO MANY PEOPLE SIMPLY WHACK THE WHOLE LOT INTO A POT OF BOILING WATER AND BLANCH THE BEJEEZUS OUT OF THEM UNTIL THEY ARE SOGGY, LIFELESS AND BLAND, AND YOU WONDER WHY KIDS HATE THEM! BUT WHEN THEY'RE COOKED CORRECTLY, THEY ARE ACTUALLY VERY

DELICIOUS AND HAVE A SUBTLE MEATY FLAVOUR — THEY ALMOST TASTE LIKE BACON! I LIKE MY BRUSSELS SPROUTS IN A SIMPLE STIR-FRY OR BAKED IN THE OVEN. THEY SHOULD BE JUST COOKED THROUGH SO THEY STILL HOLD THEIR CRUNCHINESS. THE CHARRED EDGES ARE THE BEST BITS.

Watermelon, BABY TOMATO, chèvre & CANDIED WALNUT SALAD

SERVES 4* GENEROUSLY*

THIS SALAD PRACTICALLY SHOUTS OUT 'SUMMER'! I LOVE USING FRUIT SUCH AS MANGO, POMEGRANATE OR APPLE IN SALADS, BUT FOR THIS RECIPE I HAVE CHOSEN JUICY, SWEET WATERMELON AND JAZZED IT UP WITH TOMATOES, GOAT'S CHEESE AND CANDIED WALNUTS. IT IS SO REFRESHING, AND THE SHARP FLAVOUR OF THE GOAT'S CHEESE SETS OFF THE SWEETNESS OF THE WATERMELON NICELY. THIS IS A PERFECT SUMMER SALAD THAT GOES REALLY WELL WITH BEEF, LAMB OR VENISON.

500 g (1 lb 2 oz) watermelon flesh, cut into cubes
1 × 400 g (14 oz) punnet baby roma (plum) tomatoes, halved
20 g ($\frac{3}{4}$ oz) chèvre (goat's cheese)

CANDIED WALNUTS
100 g ($3\frac{1}{2}$ oz/1 cup) walnuts
110 g ($3\frac{3}{4}$ oz/$\frac{1}{2}$ cup) sugar
1 teaspoon cayenne pepper
pinch of ground cinnamon
pinch of salt

BALSAMIC DRESSING
2 tablespoons walnut oil
1 tablespoon balsamic vinegar
juice of $\frac{1}{2}$ lemon
1 teaspoon finely chopped mint leaves
pinch of salt and pepper

1 Preheat the oven to 170°C (340°F) and line a tray with baking paper. To make the candied walnuts, place the walnuts on a baking tray and toast them in the oven for 5 minutes. Alternatively, toast the walnuts in a dry frying pan over medium heat until lightly coloured. Remove and set aside to cool.

2 Melt the sugar in a saucepan over medium heat, stirring constantly to break up any lumps. Once the sugar has fully melted and is amber in colour, add the cayenne pepper, cinnamon and salt and mix well. Quickly add the walnuts and stir to make sure all the nuts are nicely coated in the toffee.

3 Remove the pan from the heat and spread the nuts on the prepared tray to cool. Once cooled and hardened, break them into smaller pieces and keep them in an airtight container until ready to use.

4 Whisk together all the ingredients for the balsamic dressing and set aside.

5 To assemble the salad, gently combine the watermelon and tomatoes together in a mixing bowl, then transfer to a serving plate. Sprinkle with the walnuts, then crumble the chèvre over the top. Drizzle with the balsamic dressing.

Roast spiced cauliflower & CORN SALAD

SERVES
4

SOME VEGETABLES JUST AREN'T THAT INTERESTING, BUT YOU CAN MAKE THEM EXCITING ALL OVER AGAIN SIMPLY BY CHANGING THE WAY YOU COOK THEM. CAULIFLOWER IS PROBABLY NOT MY FAVOURITE VEGETABLE; NO MATTER HOW I BOILED, STEAMED OR BLANCHED THEM, THESE BUGGERS WERE DULL AND FLAVOURLESS. THEN I DISCOVERED THAT CAULIFLOWER BELONGS TO THE SAME FAMILY AS CABBAGE, BRUSSELS SPROUTS AND BROCCOLI, AND THE BEST WAY TO BRING OUT THEIR SWEET, ALMOST MEATY FLAVOUR IS TO ROAST THEM, SIMILAR TO HOW I COOK MY BRUSSELS SPROUTS (PAGE 74).

2 slices white bread, toasted (see note)
2 corn cobs, with husks
1 red capsicum (pepper)
3 tablespoons olive oil, plus extra
   to drizzle
350 g (12 oz) (half a head) cauliflower,
   cut into small florets

1 tablespoon fennel seeds, toasted
1 teaspoon cumin seeds, toasted
1 tablespoon ground turmeric
sea salt flakes
freshly ground black pepper
small handful flat-leaf (Italian)
   parsley, chopped

1 Preheat the oven to 220°C (430°F). Place the toasted bread in a small food processor and pulse a few times until it resembles coarse breadcrumbs. Set aside.

2 Preheat the barbecue grill to medium. Put the corn cobs in their husks on the grill and cook for 20–25 minutes, turning occasionally until all sides are cooked and the husks are blackened. Remove and set aside to cool. When the corn is cool enough to handle, peel the husks off and use a sharp knife to slice down the cob to cut off all the corn kernels. Transfer to a bowl and set aside for later use.

3 Meanwhile, place the capsicum on top of a gas hob over a naked flame or on the barbecue, turning frequently using kitchen tongs, and roast until the skin blackens and blisters on all sides. Put the charred capsicum inside a zip-lock bag and let it steam for 10 minutes until softened.

Rub the capsicum against the plastic bag to peel the skin off. Remove from the bag and rinse under water to remove the remaining skin, then dry and dice into small chunks. Set aside.

4 Heat the olive oil in a frying pan over medium–high heat, add the cauliflower florets, placing them cut side down, and fry for 5 minutes, or until lightly browned, then flip them over and fry for a further 2 minutes. Remove from the heat and transfer the cauliflower to a roasting tin. Add the breadcrumbs, capsicum, fennel seeds, cumin seeds and turmeric, then season with a pinch of salt and pepper and drizzle with olive oil. Give everything a quick mix with both hands, then bake for 25–30 minutes until the cauliflower is slightly wilted and browned on the edges. Remove from the oven, add the corn kernels to the tin, stir to mix well and then transfer to a serving plate. Season with extra salt and pepper and a sprinkle of chopped parsley.

Note: It's best to make your own breadcrumbs for this recipe (as described in step 1), as store-bought breadcrumbs can be too finely ground.

ROAST POTATOES, BLACK PUDDING & pork belly

SERVES 4

I ADORE DUCK FAT ROASTED POTATOES AND MANY WOULD AGREE THEY ARE INDEED THE BEST ROAST POTATOES IN THE WORLD! THE DUCK FAT MAKES THE POTATOES SUPER CRISPY ON THE OUTSIDE, LIGHT AND FLUFFY ON THE INSIDE, AND THE FLAVOUR IS EXTRAORDINARY. BUT WHAT MAKES IT EVEN MORE LUXURIOUS IS THE ADDITION OF TWO OTHER FAVOURITE FOODS OF MINE — BLACK PUDDING AND PORK BELLY. YOU CAN GET DUCK FAT FROM FINE FOOD STORES, OR RESERVE THE FAT AFTER PREPARING ANOTHER DUCK DISH, SUCH AS THE FIVE-SPICED DUCK PANCAKES ON PAGE 32.

4 coliban or sebago potatoes, peeled and cut into 2 cm ($\frac{3}{4}$ inch) cubes

60 g (2 oz/$\frac{1}{4}$ cup) duck fat (see note page 115)

2 tablespoons olive oil

1 black pudding, cut into cubes

1 large red chilli, finely chopped

handful of coriander (cilantro) leaves, roughly chopped

pinch of sea salt flakes

PORK BELLY

200 g (7 oz) pork belly, skin removed (or use 3 or 4 strips of pork spare ribs)

1 carrot, diced

1 celery stalk, diced

1 onion, diced

1 teaspoon fennel seeds

1 litre (34 fl oz/4 cups) vegetable stock

1 First prepare the pork belly. Preheat the oven to 150°C (300°F). Place the pork belly, carrot, celery, onion and fennel seeds in a small roasting tin. Pour the vegetable stock over the meat until it is fully covered. (Add more stock or water as necessary to cover the pork belly.) Cover the tin with a sheet of baking paper, pressing down so that the paper floats on top of the stock. Braise the pork belly in the oven for 3 hours.

2 Remove the tin from the oven and let the pork rest in the stock to cool down completely. Take the pork out of the stock and transfer to a tray, cover with plastic wrap and refrigerate.

3 Put the potatoes in a large saucepan, cover with cold water and bring to the boil over medium–high heat. Once boiling, reduce the heat to medium and simmer for 10 minutes, or until the potatoes are partially cooked. Drain well and set aside in the colander to dry a bit.

4 Increase the oven to 200°C (400°C). Put the duck fat in a roasting tin, then place the tin in the oven for 5 minutes, or until the fat is smoking hot. Put the potatoes in the tin and give them a quick stir to coat in the duck fat. Roast the potatoes in the oven for 25–30 minutes, or until golden and crisp. Turn once.

5 Cut the pork belly into thick chunks. When the potatoes are almost ready, heat a frying pan with the olive oil over medium heat. Add the black pudding and pork belly and fry until caramelised and crispy on the edges. Transfer to a large mixing bowl.

6 Take the potatoes out of the oven and put them into the bowl with the meat. Sprinkle with chilli and coriander leaves, season with sea salt, then toss well to combine. Transfer to a serving plate.

CHAPTER 3

BREAKFAST PIE ✦ Eggy brekky heart ✦ SMOKED HAM HOCK BAKED BEANS ✦ Kaya toast & soft-boiled eggs ✦ LAP CHEONG & SALTED RADISH OMELETTE ✦ Baked eggs with chorizo, potatoes & basil pesto ✦ PROSCIUTTO-WRAPPED CHICKEN WITH SMASHED POTATOES ✦ Cola chilli chicken ✦ AYAM PONGTEH {BRAISED POTATO CHICKEN} ✦ Ipoh bean sprouts chicken ✦ FORTY CLOVES GARLIC & TARRAGON CHICKEN WITH ROASTED VEGETABLES ✦ Mum's vinegar-braised pork belly & eggs ✦ BAKED GARLIC PORK MINCE CAKES ✦ Toad in a hole ✦ SEARED SCOTCH FILLETS WITH CHIMICHURRI SAUCE & SWEET POTATO CRISPS ✦ Thai beef mango salad with nam jim dressing ✦ BLOODY MUSSELS MARY ✦ Seared scallops & black pudding with pea purée ✦ PEPPER ASSAM PRAWNS ✦ Ocean trout with fennel, grapefruit & pomegranate salad ✦ STEAMED BLACK BEAN SNAPPER PARCELS

THESE RECIPES CAN BE EASILY PREPARED FOR A QUICK WEEKNIGHT MEAL OR A LAZY SUNDAY FEAST WITH FRIENDS. THIS CHAPTER IS PARTICULARLY SUITABLE FOR BEGINNERS WHO WOULD LIKE TO LEARN BASIC, SIMPLE, DELICIOUS COOKING. EASY PEASY, LEMON SQUEEZY!

Breakfast pie

WHO DOESN'T LIKE TO BE PAMPERED WITH BREAKFAST IN BED? MAKING BREAKFAST IN BED FOR SOMEONE SPECIAL IS A WONDERFUL GESTURE BUT IF YOU REALLY WANT TO SPOIL THEM, THEN PUT A LITTLE EXTRA EFFORT INTO BREAKFAST WITH THIS DELICIOUS BREAKFAST PIE. BACON, EGGS AND BUTTERY PUFF PASTRY — WHAT'S NOT TO LOVE?

8 short bacon slices
2 large eggs, beaten
3 tablespoons full-cream milk
handful of chives, finely chopped
handful of English spinach, roughly
    chopped

salt and pepper
1 sheet puff pastry
2 hard-boiled eggs, peeled
1 egg, lightly beaten for egg wash

1 Preheat the oven to 220°C (430°F) and place a baking tray on the middle rack of the oven. Cook the bacon in a frying pan over medium–high heat until lightly coloured, then remove and drain on paper towel.

2 Put the eggs and milk in a mixing bowl, stir to combine, then stir in the chives and spinach. Season with salt and pepper.

3 Grease a 20 × 12 cm (8 × 4½ inch) ceramic dish or baking dish. Line the dish with the puff pastry, gently pressing the pastry down so it fits in all the corners. Leave the pastry hanging over the rim of the dish.

4 To assemble, arrange 4 bacon slices in the base of the dish, then place the hard-boiled eggs on top. Pour the egg and spinach mixture into the dish, then jiggle the dish a little to get rid of any air pockets. Place the remaining bacon over the top.

5 Lift the pastry up from the longest sides and fold them towards the centre, sealing the mixture inside. Trim off the shorter ends of the pastry, then fold them inwards and press down to seal. Decorate the dish with some of the pastry offcuts. Brush the pastry with the egg wash and then use a knife to make a few incisions in the top of the pastry, to let the steam out when baking.

6 Place the pie on the hot baking tray and bake for 20 minutes, then reduce the oven to 180°C (350°F) and bake for a further 20 minutes, or until the pastry is light golden brown. Serve hot with tomato sauce (ketchup), barbecue sauce or Chilli onion jam (page 275).

EGGY brekky HEART

SERVES
4

I HAVE TO ADMIT I AM NOT A MORNING PERSON AND I DO LOVE A GOOD LIE IN, ESPECIALLY ON WEEKENDS. I LOVE WEEKENDS; YOU CAN TAKE IT EASY, FORGET ABOUT EATING HEALTHY CEREAL FOR ONCE AND INSTEAD TREAT YOURSELF WITH SOMETHING A LITTLE BIT NAUGHTY. MY PERFECT WEEKEND BRUNCH HAS TO BE FRIED EGGS WITH HOMEMADE CHILLI JAM ON TOASTED SOURDOUGH BREAD, WASHED DOWN WITH A GOOD CUP OF COFFEE. THERE'S SIMPLY NO BETTER WAY TO EXPRESS MY AFFECTION FOR BACON AND EGGS! JUST 'DON'T TELL MY HEART, MY EGGY BREKKY HEART...'

4 roma (plum) tomatoes, halved
sea salt flakes
4 tablespoons olive oil, plus extra
*   to drizzle*
8 short bacon slices
4 free-range eggs
8 slices crusty sourdough bread

1 bunch rocket (arugula) leaves
1 bunch watercress
extra-virgin olive oil
1 tablespoon balsamic vinegar
ground black pepper
8 tablespoons Chilli onion jam (page 275)
4 tablespoons Basil pesto (page 275)

1 Preheat the oven to 200°C (400°F). Put the tomatoes on a baking tray, cut side up, sprinkle with sea salt flakes, drizzle with olive oil and then bake in the oven for 20–25 minutes, or until the tomatoes are soft and lightly coloured on top, but are still holding their shape.

2 Meanwhile, heat 2 tablespoons of olive oil in a frying pan over medium–high heat and fry the bacon until crispy on the edges. Remove and place on a tray lined with paper towel to absorb the excess oil. Keep the bacon warm by placing the tray close to the cooktop.

3 Using the same frying pan, heat the remaining 2 tablespoons of oil over medium–high heat and fry the eggs for 2 minutes, or until the eggs are cooked but the yolks are still a bit runny.

4 At the same time, heat a chargrill pan over medium heat. Drizzle a little bit of olive oil on both sides of the sourdough, place in the pan and cook for 2 minutes, then flip the bread over and cook for a further 2 minutes.

5 Put the rocket leaves and watercress in a mixing bowl, drizzle with some extra-virgin olive oil and the balsamic vinegar, then season with sea salt flakes and pepper. Toss to mix well.

6 To build the brekky stack, place a small handful of salad on a slice of sourdough, top with 2 slices of roasted tomatoes, 2 pieces of bacon, a heaped spoonful of chilli jam, a fried egg and a dollop of basil pesto, then place another slice of sourdough on the side or on the top. Serve with the remaining salad.

Smoked ham hock
BAKED BEANS

I ACTUALLY DON'T KNOW ANYONE WHO MAKES BAKED BEANS FROM SCRATCH AT HOME ANYMORE. THEY CAN BE TIME CONSUMING AND A BIT EXPENSIVE TO MAKE, AND SADLY THIS DOES MAKE BUYING THOSE CANNED BAKED BEANS A LOT MORE APPEALING. BUT TASTE–WISE, HOMEMADE BAKED BEANS ARE SIMPLY UNBEATABLE, BOTH IN TERMS OF FLAVOUR AND IN THEIR RICH, ALMOST STEW-LIKE TEXTURE. I LOVE MAKING MY OWN BAKED BEANS DURING WINTER, AND I ALWAYS MAKE DOUBLE THE PORTION, SO SOME CAN BE FROZEN FOR A RAINY DAY.

400 g (14 oz) dried cannellini beans, covered with plenty of water and soaked overnight

2 tablespoons olive oil

1 large onion, finely chopped

2 carrots, finely diced

1 celery stalk, finely diced

2 garlic cloves, crushed

2 × 400 g (14 oz) tinned diced tomatoes

2 tablespoons treacle (or honey)

1 tablespoon Worcestershire sauce

1 tablespoon smoked paprika

1 bay leaf

1 smoked ham hock, skin and fat removed

salt and pepper

1 Rinse the cannellini beans, drain them and set aside.

2 Heat the olive oil in a large pot over medium heat. Add the onion, carrots and celery and sauté until the vegetables are soft and the onion is translucent. Add the garlic and cook for a further minute.

3 Add the tomatoes, treacle, Worcestershire sauce, smoked paprika and bay leaf, and stir to deglaze the pot. Put the ham hock and beans in the pot, add enough water to just cover the ingredients, then bring to the boil. Turn the heat down and simmer for 1–1½ hours, or until the beans are soft. Stir occasionally.

4 Once ready, remove the ham hock. When it is cool enough to handle, shred the meat and return it to the pot. Season with salt and pepper.

Note: The baked beans will go well with Baked eggs with chorizo (page 97). Serve on the side with the Aussie damper wagyu burger (page 156), or grab some tortillas and have a Mexican taco night!

SERVES
1*

*
(BUT
MAKES
2 JARS OF
COCONUT
JAM)

KAYA TOAST & soft-boiled EGGS

KAYA TOAST AND SOFT-BOILED EGGS GO HAND-IN-HAND, AND THIS IS A BREAKFAST STAPLE IN MALAYSIA. WHAT MAKES THIS BREAKFAST SO SPECIAL IS DEFINITELY THE KAYA JAM (SOME PEOPLE CALL IT A CUSTARD): A RICH, DARK COCONUT CURD. ACHIEVING A SILKY SMOOTH, CUSTARD-LIKE KAYA JAM DOES REQUIRE SOME ELBOW GREASE, AS YOU WILL NEED TO KEEP STIRRING THE JAM FOR A GOOD 45 MINUTES TO 1 HOUR WITHOUT LEAVING THE STOVETOP! HAVE PATIENCE MY YOUNG PADAWAN (JEDI); GOOD THINGS COME TO THOSE WHO WAIT.

2 free-range eggs, at room temperature
boiling water
2 thick slices white bread, toasted
20 g ($\frac{3}{4}$ oz) square of butter, at room temperature
dash of light soy sauce
ground white pepper

KAYA JAM
3 eggs
2 egg yolks
100 g ($3\frac{1}{2}$ oz) caster (superfine) sugar
50 g (2 oz) dark brown sugar
250 ml ($8\frac{1}{2}$ fl oz/1 cup) coconut cream
3–4 pandan (screw pine) leaves, washed (see note)

1 To make the kaya jam, put the eggs, egg yolks, caster and brown sugars in a large metal or glass mixing bowl, and beat until the sugars have dissolved.

2 Heat the coconut cream in a saucepan to boiling point, then quickly remove from the heat. Pour the hot coconut cream into the egg mixture in a slow, steady stream, stirring continuously so it doesn't curdle.

3 Stack all the pandan leaves together and tie them into a knot, then drop the leaves into the mixture. Place the metal bowl on top of a saucepan of simmering water. Using a silicone spatula, stir the egg mixture and scrape the bowl all the while to stop it curdling, until it reaches a smooth custard consistency with a nice golden brown colour — this will take about 1 hour (this is a crucial step so don't walk away). Test to see if the mixture is ready by using the 'parting the sea' technique: use the spatula to draw a line through the mixture in the bowl; if the line stays visible for a couple of seconds before the mixture flows like lava and covers the line, it is ready.

4 When the jam is cooked, it should be very thick and glossy and deep brown in colour. Remove the bowl from the heat, squeeze all the sticky jam out of the pandan leaves, then discard them. Strain the jam through a fine sieve into a jug. Leave to cool before storing in a sterilised jar. (The jam keeps well for a week at room temperature or store in the refrigerator for up to 1 month.)

5 To soft-boil the eggs, place the eggs in a small saucepan, pour in enough hot water to just cover the eggs, then cover with the lid and steam the eggs for 5 minutes. Drain off the water.

6 To serve, spread a generous layer of kaya jam on a piece of toast, place a nice thick square of butter on top, cover with the second piece of toast, then cut it in half. Crack the soft-boiled eggs into a bowl, add a dash of soy sauce and a smidgen of white pepper.

Note: Pandan leaves are available in Asian grocers, either fresh or frozen. Pandan leaves have a very subtle flavour: bruise the leaves to release the flavour by folding and tying the leaves into a knot before cooking.

LAP CHEONG & salted radish OMELETTE

4 free-range eggs
2 tablespoons water
1 tablespoon soy sauce
smidgen of ground white pepper
2 tablespoons vegetable oil
1 garlic clove, chopped
30 g (1 oz) salted radish, finely chopped (see notes)
2 lap cheong (Chinese sausages), thinly sliced (see notes)
1 spring onion (scallion), thinly sliced, plus extra for garnish
fried shallots, for garnish
Sriracha chilli sauce

1 Beat the eggs, water, soy sauce and white pepper together in a mixing bowl, then set aside.

2 Heat the vegetable oil in a non-stick frying pan over medium heat, add the garlic and salted radish and fry until fragrant. Add the lap cheong and fry until crispy on the edges.

3 Pour the beaten eggs into the pan and sprinkle the spring onion over the top. Using a spatula, gently move the egg around to make sure it is cooked evenly.

4 Fold the omelette in half and cook for a further minute, then tap the handle of the frying pan so the omelette slides to the edge of the pan, then flip the omelette over onto a plate.

5 To serve, sprinkle with fried shallots, spring onion and a splash of Sriracha chilli sauce.

Notes: Salted radish is a preserved vegetable that usually comes in a sealed packet in Asian grocers. Ask your Cantonese-speaking shop owner for 'choy bo'.

Lap cheong is also known as Chinese sausage, and is widely available in Asian grocers or the Asian ingredients aisle of major supermarkets.

I DIDN'T GROW UP EATING CHORIZO, SALAMI OR PEPPERONI BUT THEIR CLOSE CHINESE COUSIN INSTEAD, LAP CHEONG. THESE SWEETENED SUN-DRIED PORK SAUSAGES ARE A STAPLE IN MY FRIDGE; I USE THEM IN EVERYTHING FROM CHAR KUEY TEOW (PAGE 200) TO FRIED RICE (PAGE 190), OR SIMPLY STEAMED WITH A DASH OF SOY SAUCE TO GO WITH A BOWL OF RICE.

BAKED EGGS *with* chorizo, potatoes & BASIL PESTO

THIS MEXICAN BREAKFAST IS THE BEST CURE FOR A HANGOVER. THIS IS MY VERSION OF HUEVOS RANCHEROS (LITERALLY MEANING 'RANCHED EGGS'), WHICH TRADITIONALLY IS SERVED ON A TORTILLA AND USUALLY CONSISTS OF EGGS IN A CHILLI-TOMATO SAUCE, AND IS SOMETIMES SERVED WITH FRIED POTATOES (PATATAS BRAVAS) ON THE SIDE. BUT I PREFER TO KEEP IT SIMPLE AND THROW EVERYTHING INTO THE SAME PAN AND THEN BAKE IT IN THE OVEN. MAKE SURE YOU HAVE PLENTY OF TOAST TO MOP UP ALL THE SAUCE.

4 tablespoons olive oil

1 large sebago potato, peeled and cut into 1.5 cm ($\frac{5}{8}$ inch) cubes

1 chorizo sausage, sliced

1 garlic clove, crushed

$\frac{1}{2}$ onion, finely chopped

400 g (14 oz) tinned chopped tomatoes

1 teaspoon smoked paprika

salt and pepper

4 free-range eggs

2 tablespoons Basil pesto (page 275)

4 slices sourdough, toasted

1 Preheat the oven to 220°C (430°F). Heat the olive oil in a non-stick frying pan over medium heat and fry the potato cubes until golden brown with crispy edges. Add the chorizo and fry until a little charred on both sides. Add the garlic and onion and cook for a further minute until the onion is soft and translucent.

2 Add the tomatoes and smoked paprika, season with salt and pepper, and cook for 5–8 minutes, or until the sauce has reduced but is still a little sloppy. Divide the tomato and chorizo mixture between 2 small baking dishes.

3 Make two dents in the tomato mixture in each dish, then crack the eggs and gently drop them into each hole. Bake in the oven for 10 minutes, or until the eggs are just cooked through. Season with more salt and pepper, and serve with a big dollop of pesto on top, and with the toasted sourdough.

SERVES

2

THIS RECIPE IS A SIMPLE WAY TO MAKE A CHICKEN ROLL, OR 'ROULADE' AS IT IS
SOMETIMES CALLED. TECHNICALLY, MY VERSION ISN'T REALLY A ROULADE, AS
THERE ISN'T MUCH ROLLING INVOLVED, BUT THE END RESULT IS JUST AS TASTY.
APART FROM A FEW DAINTY FLOURISHES, SUCH AS WRAPPING PROSCIUTTO
AROUND THE CHICKEN AND TRUSSING IT WITH KITCHEN STRING, THE REST IS
PRETTY STRAIGHTFORWARD, ESPECIALLY THE SMASHED KIPFLER POTATOES
— JUST BOIL THEM WHOLE, SMASH, AND WHACK THEM INTO THE OVEN. I LOVE
KIPFLERS, A WAXY POTATO ALSO KNOWN AS GERMAN FINGER POTATO OR
FINGERLING, SO NAMED FOR THEIR ELONGATED SHAPE. THEY ARE USUALLY
QUITE SMALL AND HAVE A BEAUTIFUL BUTTERY, NUTTY FLAVOUR.

BE SURE TO TIME EVERYTHING WELL SO THE CHICKEN AND SMASHED POTATOES
COME OUT OF THE OVEN AT THE SAME TIME, SO THEY ARE BOTH NICE AND
WARM WHEN SERVED.

4 boneless, skinless chicken breasts
16 slices prosciutto
a few sprigs lemon thyme, leaves picked
pinch each of salt and pepper
2 tablespoons olive oil

SMASHED POTATOES
8 small kipfler (fingerling) potatoes,
   washed and unpeeled
pinch of salt
60 g (2 oz/¼ cup) duck fat (see note
   page 115)
a few sprigs lemon thyme, leaves picked

BURNT BUTTER ASPARAGUS
25 g (1 oz) unsalted butter
1 bunch asparagus (12 spears),
   ends trimmed
balsamic vinegar
salt and pepper

SERVES
4

Prosciutto-wrapped CHICKEN with SMASHED POTATOES

1 To make the smashed potatoes, put the potatoes in a pot, then fill with just enough water to cover the potatoes. Add a pinch of salt and bring to the boil over high heat. Turn the heat down to medium and boil for 15–20 minutes, or until the potatoes are cooked. Drain and transfer the potatoes to a roasting tin. Meanwhile, preheat the oven to 200°C (400°F).

2 Using a fork or potato masher, gently squash the potatoes to split them open, but still leaving large chunks. Dab the duck fat randomly on the potatoes, sprinkle with a pinch of salt and the lemon thyme, then bake for 25–30 minutes, or until the potatoes are crispy and golden brown.

3 Meanwhile, cut each chicken breast into thinner pieces by slicing it in half horizontally through the centre. Turn one half around and place the two halves back together (you should now have a log of chicken with an even thickness, with one thin end and one thick end now on top of each other). Repeat for the remaining chicken breasts.

4 For each chicken breast, lay 4 slices of prosciutto, slightly overlapping, on a clean chopping board. Place the chicken log in the centre of the prosciutto, sprinkle with the lemon thyme and season with salt and pepper. Wrap the chicken in the prosciutto, then truss firmly with kitchen string to hold it together. Repeat with the remaining chicken breasts and prosciutto.

5 Heat the olive oil in a frying pan over medium–high heat and sear the chicken on both sides until evenly golden. Transfer to a baking tray and bake at 200°C (400°F) for 12–15 minutes, or until firm to the touch.

6 Use the same pan to cook the asparagus. Melt the butter over medium heat. Once the butter starts to froth, add the asparagus and cook for 3 minutes, stirring occasionally.

7 Time it well so the chicken and roasted potatoes come out of the oven at the same time. Rest the chicken for 5 minutes, then remove the kitchen string and slice into 2 cm ($\frac{3}{4}$ inch) thick slices.

8 To serve, place 2 smashed potatoes on each plate, top with slices of chicken and the asparagus. Drizzle the asparagus with burnt butter from the pan and the balsamic vinegar, then season with salt and pepper. Serve immediately.

COLA chilli CHICKEN

THIS IS A DISH I COOKED QUITE OFTEN WHEN I WAS A POOR UNI STUDENT IN TOOWOOMBA, QUEENSLAND. I GUESS THAT'S WHAT UNI STUDENTS DO: EXPERIMENT WITH WHATEVER IS AVAILABLE IN THE PANTRY. I ADDED A LITTLE BIT OF THIS AND A LITTLE BIT OF THAT AND VOILA! — THE COLA CHILLI CHICKEN WAS BORN!

EVEN NOW, WHEN I MAKE THIS DISH FOR A COOKING DEMONSTRATION, EVERYONE GASPS IN DISBELIEF WHEN I POUR A CAN OF SOFT DRINK INTO THE WOK! WELL MY FRIENDS, BELIEVE IT OR NOT, THE SUGARY CARBONATED COLA HELPS TO TENDERISE THE CHICKEN, AND THE SWEETNESS BALANCES OUT NICELY WITH THE LIGHT AND DARK SOY SAUCES. THE SAUCE IS SO WONDERFUL THAT I SOMETIMES DRIZZLE IT OVER A BOWL OF STEAMED RICE AND CALL IT A MEAL!

500 g (1 lb 2 oz) boneless, skinless chicken thighs

1 tablespoon cornflour (cornstarch)

4 tablespoons light soy sauce

2 tablespoons vegetable oil

1 red chilli, thinly sliced

5 cm (2 inch) piece ginger, peeled and cut into 1 mm ($\frac{1}{16}$ inch) strips

3 garlic cloves, roughly chopped

355 ml (12 fl oz) can cola drink

2 tablespoons dark soy sauce

1 spring onion (scallion), cut into 5 cm (2 inch) lengths

handful of unsalted cashew nuts, toasted

1 Cut the chicken thighs into bite-sized pieces and put in a bowl. Add the cornflour and 2 tablespoons of the light soy sauce and mix well. Place the chicken in the refrigerator to marinate for at least 1 hour.

2 Heat the vegetable oil in a frying pan or wok over medium–high heat. Add the chicken and cook until browned all over, then add the chilli, ginger and garlic, and cook for another minute.

3 Pour the cola into the frying pan, adding just enough to cover the chicken; the cola will fizz up. Add the dark soy sauce and the remaining light soy sauce and let it simmer for about 15 minutes or so, until the sauce has reduced to a syrupy consistency. It should be thick and sticky.

4 Turn the heat off, add the spring onion and toasted cashews and give it a quick stir before serving. Serve with steamed jasmine rice.

Ayam pongteh
{BRAISED POTATO CHICKEN}

THIS DISH BRINGS BACK A LOT OF CHILDHOOD MEMORIES. MY MUM USED TO COOK THIS QUITE OFTEN, AS IT IS EASY TO MAKE AND DOESN'T NEED THAT MANY INGREDIENTS. AYAM PONGTEH IS A SIMPLE BRAISED CHICKEN AND POTATO STEW THAT IS SO COMFORTING AND HOMELY. WHENEVER I COOK THIS DISH, I LIKE TO KEEP SOME IN THE REFRIGERATOR AND REHEAT IT THE NEXT DAY, ONCE THE FLAVOUR HAS HAD TIME TO DEVELOP OVERNIGHT.

7–8 dried shiitake mushrooms

10 French shallots, peeled

6–8 garlic cloves, peeled

5 cm (2 inch) piece ginger, peeled

3 tablespoons vegetable oil

3 tablespoons soya bean paste (see notes)

½ chicken (500 g/1 lb 2 oz), cut into small pieces (see notes)

2 potatoes, peeled and quartered

4 tablespoons light soy sauce

1 tablespoon dark soy caramel

1 tablespoon shaved palm sugar (gula melaka) (see note on page 255)

1 Soak the shiitake mushrooms in a bowl of hot water for 1 hour until softened, then drain, reserving 375 ml (13 fl oz/1½ cups) of the mushroom water for later use. Remove and discard the mushroom stalks.

2 Put the shallots, garlic and ginger in a food processor and process to form a paste. Heat the vegetable oil in a wok or large pot over medium–high heat and fry the paste until fragrant and lightly browned. Add the soya bean paste and fry for 2–3 minutes, stirring constantly.

3 Add the chicken pieces to the wok and cook, stirring constantly, for 3 minutes, until the chicken is half cooked and well coated in the paste. Add the potatoes and mushrooms and cook for 2 minutes. Add the reserved mushroom soaking water, soy sauce, soy caramel and palm sugar. Give everything a quick stir and bring to the boil, then reduce the heat to medium–low and cook for 30 minutes, or until the sauce is thick and the potatoes are soft but not mushy.

Notes: Soya bean paste is available from Asian grocers. Alternatively, you can substitute with Korean fermented bean paste (doenjang) or Japanese miso paste, but the flavour won't be quite the same.

Instead of using half a chicken, you can substitute with chicken pieces such as breasts, drumsticks, wings or marylands. You can also use pork for this recipe.

Ipoh BEAN SPROUTS CHICKEN

1.5 kg (3 lb 5 oz) free-range whole chicken

3 garlic cloves, with skins on

5 slices of ginger

2 spring onions (scallions), white part only

1 teaspoon black peppercorns

3 tablespoons light soy sauce, plus extra to serve

1 tablespoon sesame oil, plus extra to serve

1 kg (2 lb 3 oz) fresh flat rice noodles

STOCK

5 slices of ginger

1 teaspoon black peppercorns

1 spring onion (scallion), cut into 10 cm (4 inch) lengths

3 garlic cloves, with skins on

pinch of ground white pepper

20 g ($\frac{3}{4}$ oz) dried anchovies, soaked in water for 30 minutes then drained

95 g ($3\frac{1}{2}$ oz/$\frac{1}{2}$ cup) dried soya beans

1 tablespoon salt, plus extra for seasoning

BEAN SPROUTS

250 g (9 oz) bean sprouts

2 tablespoons light soy sauce

1 teaspoon sesame oil

GARNISHES

ground white pepper

2 spring onions (scallions), thinly sliced

fried shallots

1 large red chilli, thinly sliced

IF I HAD TO NAME ONE DISH THAT REPRESENTS MY HOMETOWN, IT WOULD BE THIS ONE. I GREW UP IN THE CITY OF IPOH, IN MALAYSIA, ABOUT TWO AND A HALF HOURS' DRIVE NORTH OF KUALA LUMPUR. IPOH IS LOCATED ON TOP OF A LARGE KARSTIC FORMATION, AND THE WATER FROM THE LIMESTONE DEPOSITS THAT SEEPS INTO THE GROUND IS THOUGHT TO ACCOUNT FOR THE REGION'S TASTY FOOD, SUCH AS IPOH'S FAMOUS NOODLES, SAR HOR FUN (FLAT RICE NOODLES) — FLAWLESS, SMOOTH-AS-SILK RICE NOODLES. EVEN THE BEAN SPROUTS IN IPOH ARE EXTRA FAT AND CRUNCHY!

THIS IS A VERY SIMPLE DISH TO PREPARE AND ALL YOU NEED IS PATIENCE. THE CHICKEN IS STEEPED IN A WATER BATH THEN DUNKED INTO COLD WATER TO STOP THE COOKING PROCESS, SO THE CHICKEN REMAINS MOIST AND SUCCULENT. THE CHICKEN IS USUALLY SERVED WITH A BOWL OF NOODLE SOUP AND BLANCHED BEAN SPROUTS. THE SIMPLICITY AND CLEAN FLAVOURS OF THIS DISH EMPHASISE THE QUALITY OF THE INGREDIENTS USED.

1 To make the stock, fill a large stockpot about three-quarters full with water (there needs to be enough water to submerge the whole chicken). Add all the stock ingredients and bring to the boil.

2 Meanwhile, stuff the cavity of the chicken with the garlic cloves, ginger, spring onions and black peppercorns.

3 Once the stock water is boiling, turn off the heat. Carefully dunk the whole chicken into the stock, breast side down, and slowly let the cavity fill with stock. Put the lid on and leave the chicken in the stock for 1 hour.

4 Lift the chicken out of the stock and set aside on a tray. Bring the pot of stock to the boil again, then turn off the heat and put the chicken back in for a 45-minute bath. The chicken should be cooked by now.

5 Lift the chicken out of the stock and dunk it into a large bowl of iced water to stop the cooking process. Leave the chicken in the water for 10 minutes, or until it has cooled down completely. Drain, discard all the solids in the cavity, then pat dry with paper towel and place on a tray. Combine the soy sauce and sesame oil, then rub the mixture all over the chicken a few times until it has a nice light tan. Loosely cover with foil and set aside to rest.

6 Once again, bring the stock back to the boil over medium heat. Season with salt; now it should be a flavoursome soup stock. To prepare the bean sprouts, put them in a wire mesh ladle or sieve, drop it into the hot stock and scald for 15 seconds. Remove and shake off the excess water, then place the bean sprouts on a serving plate. Drizzle with the soy sauce and sesame oil, and garnish with white pepper, some spring onion and fried shallots.

7 Chop the chicken up using a cleaver into friendly bite-sized pieces and transfer to a serving platter. Drizzle with a dash of sesame oil and a few good splashes of soy sauce. Sprinkle with a good smidgen of white pepper and garnish with spring onion, red chilli and fried shallots.

8 To make the rice noodle soup, cook a handful of rice noodles using a wire mesh noodle strainer or a sieve in the same pot of soup stock for 1 minute. Strain, then place in a bowl. Repeat for the remaining noodles, cooking one portion at a time. Adjust the flavour of the stock with soy sauce, then ladle the hot soup over the noodles in the bowls. Sprinkle with a good pinch of white pepper and garnish with chilli, some spring onion and fried shallots. Place the chicken platter, bean sprouts and bowls of noodle soup on the table.

THIS IS CLASSIC FRENCH COMFORT FOOD AND A RECIPE THAT I WAS INSPIRED TO MAKE AFTER WATCHING ONE OF MY FOOD IDOLS, NIGELLA LAWSON, PREPARE IT ON TV. JUST HOW DOES NIGELLA MANAGE TO STILL LOOK SO EFFORTLESSLY SEXY WHILE STUFFING A CHICKEN CAVITY WITH FORTY CLOVES OF GARLIC?

SERVES
4-6

Forty cloves garlic & TARRAGON CHICKEN
WITH ROASTED VEGETABLES

3 garlic bulbs
1.5 kg (3 lb 5 oz) free-range
  whole chicken
50 g (2 oz) butter, softened
salt and freshly ground
  black pepper
3 sprigs tarragon
olive oil

ROASTED VEGETABLES
1 bunch Dutch (baby)
  carrots
6 baby onions, peeled
2 parsnips, peeled and
  quartered lengthwise
6 small beetroots, unpeeled,
  washed and halved

DON'T BE AFRAID OF THE NUMBER OF GARLIC CLOVES USED IN THIS RECIPE, BECAUSE THE FLAVOUR OF THE GARLIC MELLOWS AND SWEETENS AFTER ROASTING. SQUEEZE THE ROASTED GARLIC OVER THE VEGIES OR CHICKEN FOR EXTRA FLAVOUR. LEFTOVERS CAN BE STORED IN A JAR FILLED WITH OIL AND SPRIGS OF THYME, TO USE ON PIZZA, PASTA OR BREAD.

1 Preheat the oven to 200°C (400°F). Give the whole garlic bulbs a good whack using the palm of your hand to separate the cloves. It doesn't matter if you have more than 40 garlic cloves — who's counting?

2 Place the chicken on a chopping board with the cavity facing you, and gently push your fingers through the gap under the skin to loosen it from the breasts. Rub half of the butter on the breasts underneath the skin. Rub some salt and pepper inside the cavity, then stuff it with the tarragon sprigs and half of the garlic cloves (you can leave the skin on the garlic cloves). Truss the chicken to close the cavity.

3 Rub the remaining butter all over the chicken, then season with salt and pepper, and give the chicken a good massage.

4 Place the remaining garlic cloves in a roasting dish, drizzle with some olive oil, then place the chicken on top. Roast the chicken in the oven for 1 hour 20 minutes, or until the chicken is tender and the juices run clear when the thigh is pierced with a skewer.

5 Meanwhile, prepare your vegetables and put them in another roasting dish. Drizzle with olive oil, then put the dish on the bottom rack in the oven for the last 45 minutes of cooking.

6 Once cooked, transfer the chicken to a serving platter and surround it with the roasted garlic and vegetables. Let the meat rest for 15 minutes before carving. Serve the roast chicken with the garlic cloves; squeeze the soft mellow garlic flesh out of the skins.

WHAT IS YOUR FAVOURITE DISH THAT YOUR MUM COOKS FOR YOU? MY MUM'S VINEGAR-BRAISED PORK BELLY WITH HARD-BOILED EGGS IS HANDS DOWN MY FAVOURITE DISH OF ALL TIME. EVERY TIME I GO HOME TO VISIT MY FAMILY IN MALAYSIA, I SPECIFICALLY PUT IN A REQUEST FOR MUM TO COOK THIS FOR ME. THE SLOW-BRAISED PORK BELLY SIMPLY MELTS IN THE MOUTH AND THE STAR ANISE GIVES IT A DISTINCTIVE AROMATIC ANISEED FLAVOUR. I LIKE TO COOK THIS DURING WINTER AND ON RAINY DAYS; IT IS SO COMFORTING AND HEALS ALL MY HOMESICKNESS.

MUM'S vinegar-braised PORK BELLY & Eggs

2 litres (68 fl oz/8 cups) water

500 g (1 lb 2 oz) pork spare ribs, chopped into 2.5–5 cm (1–2 inch) pieces (see note)

500 g (1 lb 2 oz) pork belly, skin off, cut into 3 cm (1¼ inch) cubes

5 cm (2 inch) piece ginger, peeled and thinly sliced

1 garlic bulb

10 star anise

5 dried chillies (optional)

3 tablespoons white vinegar

3 tablespoons dark soy caramel

100 ml (3½ fl oz) light soy sauce

220 g (7¾ oz/1 cup) sugar

6 hard-boiled eggs, peeled (extra for the egg lovers)

1 Pour the water into a large non-stainless steel pot (such as a large Chinese claypot or enamelled cast-iron casserole dish), and bring to the boil over medium–high heat.

2 Add the pork ribs and pork belly to the boiling water, then add the ginger slices, the whole garlic bulb, star anise and chillies (if using), and bring back to the boil. Scoop out all the impurities floating on the surface.

3 Turn the heat down to a simmer, then add the vinegar, dark soy caramel, light soy sauce and sugar. Give it all a stir until the sugar has dissolved, then add the hard-boiled eggs. Braise the pork for at least 2 hours, or until the pork is meltingly tender, stirring occasionally.

4 When the sauce starts to thicken, have a taste and adjust the seasoning accordingly. If it is too sour or too salty, add a little more sugar. If it is too sweet, add more light soy sauce. Do not add more water unless it dries out too quickly. Serve hot with a bowl of steamed jasmine rice.

Note: You can buy pork spare ribs in major supermarkets. If not, ask your butcher to cut up a whole piece of pork belly with bones left in.

THIS IS ANOTHER DISH THAT I LIKE TO COOK IN A MUFFIN TRAY (THE OTHER RECIPE IS TOAD IN THE HOLE, PAGES 114–115). THE MINCE CAKES WILL NOT ONLY COOK FASTER IN THE INDIVIDUAL MUFFIN HOLES, BUT THIS ALSO ENABLES YOU TO KEEP THE PORTION SIZE IN CHECK. NOT TO MENTION THAT THESE ARE SUPER DUPER, EASY BREEZY TO MAKE.

THE MINCE CAKES HAVE A NICE ELASTIC TEXTURE, ACHIEVED FROM THE 'SLAPPING' TECHNIQUE, AND IF YOU LOVE GARLIC THEN THESE ARE RIGHT UP YOUR ALLEY. I LIKE TO SERVE THEM WITH LOTS OF XO SAUCE, BUT YOU CAN ALWAYS JUST GIVE THEM A GOOD SPLASH OF SOY SAUCE OR CHILLI SAUCE. I LIKE TO CALL THESE THE 'RISSOLES OF THE EAST'.

MAKES 6

500 g (1 lb 2 oz) minced (ground) pork
3 garlic cloves, finely chopped
10 g ($\frac{1}{2}$ oz) salted radish, rinsed and finely chopped (see note page 94)
1 egg, beaten
2 tablespoons light soy sauce
1 teaspoon five-spice powder
pinch of white pepper
6 teaspoons vegetable oil
XO sauce, as dressing (page 273)
handful of coriander (cilantro) leaves, roughly chopped
handful of fried shallots

1 Preheat the oven to 220°C (430°F). In a large mixing bowl, combine the pork, garlic, salted radish, egg, soy sauce, five-spice and white pepper.

2 Pick up all the mixture in one hand and then slap it against the side of the bowl for 5 minutes until the meat is sticky. This technique is to break down the meat fibres, so that it will have a nice elastic texture once cooked.

3 Divide the mixture into 6 equal portions. Have ready a 6-hole muffin tray. Place one portion into each hole, pressing down to fit tightly in the holes. Drizzle a teaspoon of vegetable oil over each mince cake, then bake in the oven for 20 minutes.

4 Remove from the oven and transfer the mince cakes to serving plates. Drizzle with a generous amount of XO sauce and sprinkle liberally with coriander leaves and fried shallots. Serve with steamed rice as a meal.

Baked garlic
PORK MINCE CAKES

NO, WE ARE NOT JUST CUTTING A BIG HOLE IN A SLICE OF BREAD AND COOKING AN EGG IN IT — WE ARE MAKING THE CLASSIC ENGLISH TOAD IN A HOLE, MADE WITH SAUSAGES IN YORKSHIRE PUDDING. THE RECIPE ITSELF IS SIMPLE BUT IT DOES REQUIRE SOME SKILL TO COOK IT PERFECTLY; IT TOOK ME MANY ATTEMPTS TO ACHIEVE A RESULT I WAS FINALLY HAPPY WITH. MY BEST TIP IS TO USE AN OIL WITH A HIGH SMOKING POINT, LIKE DUCK FAT OR VEGETABLE SHORTENING, AS THIS WILL GIVE YOU A NICE CRISPY CRUST ON YOUR YORKSHIRE PUDDING. BUT A FINAL WORD OF WARNING: THESE ARE SERIOUSLY DELICIOUS BUT THEY ARE NOT VERY WAISTLINE-FRIENDLY!

MAKES
6

Toad IN A HOLE

6 short gourmet
   sausages
vegetable oil
75 g (2½ oz/½ cup) plain
   (all-purpose) flour
1 egg
250 ml (8½ fl oz/1 cup)
   full-cream milk

3 sprigs thyme, leaves
   picked
salt and pepper
3 tablespoons lard or
   duck fat, at room
   temperature (see note)
mustard and gravy, to
   serve (optional)

1 Preheat the oven to 220°C (430°F). Fry the sausages in a pan with a little bit of oil until half cooked — about 3 minutes on each side. Remove and set aside.

2 Sift the flour into a bowl, make a well in the centre, then break the egg into it. Pour the milk in a steady stream into the bowl, stirring to gradually incorporate the flour into the mixture until it forms a smooth batter. Pass the batter through a fine sieve into a jug to make sure it is lump free. Add the thyme leaves and season well with salt and pepper.

3 Have ready a 6-hole muffin tray. Drizzle 2 teaspoons of fat into each hole, then place the tray in the oven for 5 minutes, or until the fat is smoking hot.

4 For this step, I find it's best to open the oven door and pull the oven rack and muffin tray out a bit, without removing it from the oven so the oil stays as hot as possible. Carefully pour the batter into each hole until half full, then place a sausage into each one. Put the tray back in the oven and bake for 20–25 minutes, or until the batter is puffed up, golden brown and crispy. Serve with mustard and gravy if you like.

Note: You can buy duck fat at delicatessens or fine food stores, or rendered from another duck recipe (page 32). Duck fat stores well in the refrigerator and will keep for several months. Alternatively, substitute the duck fat with oil that has a high smoking point, such as sunflower oil, canola oil or vegetable shortening.

SEARED SCOTCH FILLETS with CHIMICHURRI SAUCE & sweet potato crisps

I CAME FROM A COUNTRY WHERE PEOPLE BELIEVE MEAT SHOULD ALWAYS BE 110 PER CENT COOKED THROUGH UNTIL IT IS LIFELESS, GREY AND BONE DRY. ONLY AFTER MOVING TO AUSTRALIA HAVE I LEARNT HOW TO APPRECIATE AND COOK A GOOD STEAK. AFTER MANY ATTEMPTS AND MANY MEDIOCRE STEAKS WITH BLOOD JUICES LEAKING ALL OVER THE PLATE, I HAVE COME TO REALISE THAT RESTING THE STEAK BEFORE SERVING IS JUST AS IMPORTANT AS COOKING IT.

MY BEST ADVICE IS TO BUY A GREAT CUT OF MEAT, SUCH AS RIB EYE. IT MIGHT BE A LITTLE BIT MORE EXPENSIVE, BUT I LIKE TO THINK THAT IF I HAD ORDERED IT FROM A RESTAURANT, IT WOULD HAVE COST ME AN ARM AND A LEG — SO BUYING A GOOD STEAK FROM MY LOCAL BUTCHER AND COOKING IT MYSELF AT HOME IS REALLY QUITE A BARGAIN!

1 orange sweet potato, peeled

vegetable oil, for deep-frying

4 × 250 g (9 oz) scotch fillets (rib eye steaks)

salt and pepper

olive oil

Chimichurri sauce, to serve (page 272)

1 To make the sweet potato crisps, peel the sweet potato into thin strips using a vegetable peeler.

2 Pour the vegetable oil into a small saucepan until about half full, then heat the oil to 180°C (350°F) over medium–high heat. Test to see if the oil is hot enough by dipping a wooden chopstick in the oil — if the oil starts steadily bubbling around the chopstick, it's ready. Working in batches, fry the sweet potato strips until crispy; the potato crisps will stop sizzling rapidly once they are ready. Remove and drain on paper towel.

3 Preheat the barbecue grill or a chargrill pan to medium–high. Season the steaks liberally with salt and pepper, and drizzle with olive oil on both sides. Cook the steaks for 6–7 minutes on each side, then remove from the heat and set aside to rest for 5 minutes.

4 Slice the meat and fan it out on a serving plate. Serve topped with a generous amount of chimichurri sauce and a mound of sweet potato crisps on the side.

SERVES 4

Thai beef MANGO SALAD with NAM JIM dressing

100 g (3½ oz) dried rice vermicelli noodles

600 g (1 lb 5 oz) rump steak

salt and pepper

olive oil

2 Lebanese (short) cucumbers, halved, seeded and thinly sliced

1 large ripe mango, peeled and thinly sliced

small handful of mint leaves

small handful of coriander (cilantro) leaves

125 ml (4 fl oz/½ cup) Nam jim dressing (page 270)

40 g (1½ oz/¼ cup) unsalted peanuts, toasted and roughly chopped

small handful of fried shallots

1 Put the rice noodles in a heatproof bowl and pour over enough boiling water to fully submerge the noodles. Soak for 30 minutes, or until softened, then drain.

2 Preheat the barbecue hotplate or grill until smoking hot. Season the steak with salt and pepper on both sides, then drizzle with olive oil. Grill the steak for 4–5 minutes on each side for medium–rare. Remove from the heat and place on a plate, then cover and let the steak rest for 10 minutes. Slice into thin strips.

3 To serve, place the beef, cucumber, mango, noodles, mint and coriander leaves in a large mixing bowl, and toss to combine. Transfer the salad to serving plates, drizzle with nam jim dressing and sprinkle with toasted peanuts and fried shallots.

SERVES
4

MANGO IS MY ABSOLUTE FAVOURITE FRUIT TO EAT. THIS COLD NOODLE SALAD IS A GREAT ONE FOR SUMMER WHEN MANGOES ARE IN SEASON. I LOVE HOW THE SWEETNESS OF THE MANGO BRINGS A WHOLE NEW DIMENSION OF FLAVOUR AND A BIT OF A SUMMERY TWIST TO THE TRADITIONAL THAI BEEF SALAD.

BLOODY MUSSELS *Mary*

MUSSELS ARE THE MOST UNDERRATED SEAFOOD IN THE WORLD, PARTICULARLY IN AUSTRALIA. MUSSELS ARE INEXPENSIVE; THEY ARE A GOOD SOURCE OF PROTEIN, IRON, IODINE AND OMEGA-3; THEY ARE EASY TO PREPARE AND GO WELL WITH A VARIETY OF FLAVOURS; AND THEY ARE PERFECT FOR A CASUAL LUNCH WITH A GROUP OF FRIENDS OVER FOR A FEW BEERS. SO WHY DON'T WE EAT MORE OF THEM?

WHEN BUYING MUSSELS, I FIND KINKAWOOKA MUSSELS ARE THE BEST WHEN IT COMES TO FRESHNESS AND FLAVOUR. THEY USUALLY COME ALREADY SCRUBBED, AND BEARDED IN A SEALED BAG, SO ALL YOU HAVE TO DO IS JUST THROW THEM INTO A LARGE POT OF FLAVOURSOME BROTH AND POP THE LID ON. BUT WHETHER THEY ARE BLUE MUSSELS FROM AUSTRALIA OR GREEN MUSSELS FROM NEW ZEALAND, JUST MAKE SURE THE MUSSELS ARE GROWN AND HARVESTED FROM A HEALTHY, SUSTAINABLE ENVIRONMENT.

2 tablespoons olive oil

1 onion, finely diced

3 garlic cloves, roughly chopped

½ celery stalk, finely diced

50 g (2 oz) speck (or bacon), cut into thin strips

400 g (14 oz) tinned diced tomatoes

1 teaspoon Tabasco sauce

1 tablespoon Worcestershire sauce

3 tablespoons vodka

1 kg (2 lb 3 oz) black mussels, scrubbed and bearded

handful of parsley, roughly chopped

½ lemon

1 Heat the olive oil in a big pot over medium heat. Add the onion, garlic and celery and sauté for about 5 minutes, or until the onion is soft and translucent. Add the speck and fry until crispy on the edges.

2 Add the tomatoes, Tabasco sauce, Worcestershire sauce and vodka, then stir well and bring to the boil. Once boiling, put all the mussels into the pot, quickly put the lid on and let them steam for 4 minutes, shaking the pot every now and again. The mussels are ready once they have all opened.

3 Tip the mussels into a large serving bowl, sprinkle with the parsley and squeeze over the lemon juice.

SEARED SCALLOPS
& black pudding
with pea purée

NO, NO! THIS RECIPE IS IN THE RIGHT CHAPTER. LOOKS IMPRESSIVE, NO? WELL, IT LOOKS MORE COMPLICATED THAN IT ACTUALLY IS. THIS IS A GREAT ENTRÉE DISH FOR DINNER PARTIES, BUT YOU DO HAVE TO BUY THE FRESHEST SCALLOPS AND THE BEST BLACK PUDDING YOU CAN FIND. AND TAKE YOUR TIME WITH THE PRESENTATION, AS EVERY SINGLE DETAIL MAKES A HUGE DIFFERENCE. YOUR GUESTS WILL THINK THAT YOU HAVE PUT A LOT OF EFFORT INTO PREPARING THIS BEAUTIFUL DISH.

SERVES 4

4 slices prosciutto
150 g (5 oz/1½ cups) fresh or frozen peas
20 g (¾ oz) butter for the peas, plus 40 g (1½ oz) extra for the scallops
1 pear, such as Green Anjou or Bartlett, unpeeled

1 tablespoon lemon juice
2 tablespoons olive oil
12 thick slices black pudding
12 scallops, roe removed
salt and freshly ground black pepper

1 Preheat the oven to 180°C (350°F). Put the prosciutto on a baking tray lined with baking paper, then place another baking tray on the top to stack them together. This will prevent the prosciutto from curling as it cooks. Transfer the trays to the oven and bake for 15 minutes. Remove from the oven and cool on the tray, then break the crisp prosciutto into long, thin strips.

2 Fill a small saucepan with water until about one-third full and bring to the boil. Add a pinch of salt and then the peas. Reduce the heat and simmer for 5 minutes, or until the peas are tender. Drain the peas, reserving 2 tablespoons of the cooking liquid. Place the peas, reserved liquid and 20 g (¾ oz) butter into a small food processor and purée until smooth. Pass the purée through a fine sieve into a bowl. Pour the pea purée into a squeeze bottle and refrigerate.

3 Using a mandolin, thinly slice the pear and place in a bowl. Drizzle with the lemon juice and toss well to prevent oxidation. Cover and refrigerate.

4 Heat the olive oil in a frying pan, add the black pudding and fry for 2 minutes on each side. Remove and keep warm in the oven (the oven should still be a little warm from cooking the prosciutto).

5 Season the scallops with salt and pepper. Wipe the frying pan clean, then add 40 g (1½ oz) butter and melt it over high heat. Once the butter is frothing, add the scallops and sear for 2 minutes on one side, then turn them over and sear for 1 minute on the other side.

6 Allow 3 scallops and 3 slices of black pudding per person. To serve, squeeze dollops of pea purée on the plate, add the black pudding and top with the scallops. Garnish with pear slices and prosciutto strips, and sprinkle a trail of ground black pepper on the side.

PEPPER *Assam* PRAWNS

ASSAM PRAWNS, OR TAMARIND PRAWNS, IS ONE OF MY FAVOURITE NYONYA SEAFOOD DISHES. THERE ARE MANY VERSIONS MADE WITH DIFFERENT STYLES OF TAMARIND SAUCE, BUT I PREFER THE DRY VERSION AS IT HAS AN INTENSE SOURNESS FROM THE TAMARIND SAUCE THAT ACCENTUATES THE SWEETNESS OF THE PRAWNS. USE YOUR FINGERS TO PICK UP THE PRAWNS AND SUCK ALL THE SWEET AND SOUR JUICES ON THE SHELLS BEFORE PEELING THEM — THAT'S THE BEAUTY OF EATING PRAWNS WITH SHELLS ON. PREPARE A BOWL OF WATER WITH A FEW LIME WEDGES IN IT, TO WASH YOUR STICKY FINGERS AFTERWARDS.

500 g (1 lb 2 oz) raw prawns (shrimp)

1 teaspoon salt

2 tablespoons tamarind pulp

125 ml (4 fl oz/½ cup) hot water

vegetable oil, for deep-frying

1 teaspoon sesame oil

1 tablespoon dark soy caramel

1 tablespoon sugar

1 tablespoon freshly ground black pepper

1 Trim the prawns' legs with scissors, then cut along the spine and remove the intestinal tract. Rinse the prawns and place in a bowl. Add the salt and mix well, then fill the bowl with water until the prawns are fully submerged. Cover and place in the refrigerator for 30 minutes.

2 Soak the tamarind pulp in the hot water for 10 minutes. Strain the tamarind liquid into a bowl, pressing the pulp with a wooden spoon to extract all the tamarind paste. Discard the seeds and pulp.

3 Remove the prawns from the refrigerator, rinse and pat dry with paper towel. Pour the vegetable oil into a wok until about half full, then heat the oil to 190°C (375°F over medium–high heat. Test to see if the oil is hot enough by dipping a wooden chopstick into the hot oil — if the oil starts steadily bubbling around the chopstick, it's ready. Working in batches, deep-fry the prawns for 3 minutes until golden brown. Remove and drain on paper towel.

4 Pour the hot oil out of the wok, and reserve 2 tablespoons of oil. Wipe the wok clean, then heat it up again with the reserved oil. Pour in the tamarind water, sesame oil and dark soy caramel, season with sugar and black pepper, then simmer until the liquid has reduced by half. Return the prawns to the wok, stirring well to make sure they are well coated in the sauce. Serve with steamed rice.

SERVES

4

OCEAN TROUT WITH
fennel, grapefruit
& POMEGRANATE SALAD

I FIND THE BEST WAY TO COOK OCEAN TROUT IS TO SIMPLY SEASON WITH SALT AND PEPPER, PAN-FRY ON THE SKIN SIDE UNTIL CRISPY, THEN FLIP IT OVER AND QUICKLY SEAR UNTIL JUST COOKED. FOR THIS RECIPE, YOU CAN SUBSTITUTE THE TROUT WITH SALMON OR ANY MEATY WHITE FISH LIKE MONKFISH OR LING FISH. A CITRUSY, ANISE-FLAVOURED SALAD ALWAYS GOES WELL WITH FISH. AND MANDARIN, BLOOD ORANGE, DILL AND ASPARAGUS ARE ALL GOOD ALTERNATIVES FOR THIS RECIPE.

2 fennel bulbs
juice of 1 lime
1 grapefruit
½ pomegranate
salt and pepper
2 tablespoons olive oil
4 ocean trout fillets, skin on, pin-boned
extra-virgin olive oil
sea salt flakes

SERVES 4

1 Cut the tops off the fennel, saving the leafy green fronds for garnishing. Use a mandolin slicer, with the flat side of the fennel facing the blade, and slice the fennel very thinly. Put the shaved fennel in a bowl and mix with the lime juice to stop oxidation. Peel the grapefruit, removing the bitter white pith, then use a small knife to slice between the membranes to remove each segment. Put the grapefruit segments in the bowl with the fennel.

2 Bash the back of the pomegranate with a wooden spoon until the seeds fall out. Pick out all the white pith and discard it, then add the juicy red seeds to the fennel and grapefruit. Season with salt and pepper, and set aside.

3 Heat the olive oil in a frying pan over medium heat. Season the trout with salt and pepper, then cook, skin side down, for 2–3 minutes, or until the skin is crisp. Turn the fish over and cook for a further 2 minutes, or until cooked to your liking.

4 To serve, place a handful of salad on each plate, top with a piece of trout, drizzle with extra-virgin olive oil and sprinkle with sea salt flakes. Scatter over some chopped fennel fronds for garnish.

Steamed BLACK BEAN snapper parcels

SOMETIMES I DO HAVE THOSE MOMENTS WHERE I JUST CAN'T BE BOTHERED TO MUCK AROUND IN THE KITCHEN AFTER A BUSY DAY, AND THIS RECIPE USUALLY COMES TO THE RESCUE. A GREAT WAY TO COOK FISH IS SIMPLY BY WRAPPING IT UP IN BAKING PAPER AND THEN JUST POPPING IT INTO THE OVEN TO LET IT DO ITS THING. NO FUSS!

8 dried shiitake mushrooms
5 cm (2 inch) piece ginger, peeled and cut into thin strips
4 × 160 g (5½ oz) snapper fillets
150 g (5 oz) Chinese salted black bean paste (see note)
1 large red chilli, finely chopped
2 tablespoons mirin
3 tablespoons Shaoxing rice wine
125 ml (4 fl oz/½ cup) olive oil
2 garlic cloves, finely chopped
2 teaspoons sesame oil
3 tablespoons light soy sauce
2 spring onions (scallions), thinly sliced

Note: *Chinese salted black bean paste is available from Asian grocers. It is more concentrated than the black bean sauce that comes in a bottle.*

1 Soak the shiitake mushrooms in a bowl of hot water for 1 hour until softened, then drain. Remove and discard the mushroom stalks, then slice into thin strips.

2 Preheat the oven to 170°C (340°F). Cut out four 30 cm (12 inch) circles from sheets of baking paper. Use good-quality baking paper so it won't tear easily; if not use two circles for each parcel (you will then need to cut out another four circles).

3 Divide the mushroom and ginger into 4 portions. Place one portion in the middle of each paper circle, then top with a fish fillet.

4 Mix the black bean paste, chilli, mirin and rice wine together in a bowl. Spread 2 tablespoons of the mixture on top of each fillet. Fold the sides of the paper over the fish to meet in the middle, then pleat the paper to seal the fish in. Place the parcels on a baking tray and bake in the oven for 15 minutes.

5 Meanwhile, heat the olive oil in a saucepan over medium heat and fry the garlic until golden brown and crispy. Remove from the heat and add the sesame oil and soy sauce.

6 Place the fish in their paper parcels on serving plates. Drizzle a tablespoon of soy sauce dressing over the fish, then garnish with the fried garlic and spring onion.

SERVES
4

over
THE TOP

Yee sang • A LITTLE BEET OF THIS AND A LITTLE BEET OF THAT • Nyonya devil curry • MARMITE CHICKEN • Buddha's bowl • ROAST DUCK & LYCHEE RED CURRY • Perfect roast pork belly in apple cider • PULLED PORK & ACAR AWAK LETTUCE WRAP • Twice-cooked pork belly with apple & cabbage slaw • AUSSIE DAMPER WAGYU BURGER • Beef rendang • BEEF CHEEKS BOURGUIGNON WITH CAULIFLOWER & LEEK PURÉE • Osso bucco with soft polenta & corn • RIBS YOUR HEART OUT • Slow-roast lamb shoulder with rosemary & preserved lemon • LAMB SHANK PIE • Cereal butter prawns • NYONYA SPICY TAMARIND SNAPPER • Deep-fried soft shell crab with som tum • IKAN PARI PAKAR {GRILLED SPICY SKATE WING IN BANANA LEAF} • Burnt butter lobster tail with apple & salmon roe • GOLDEN SAND MUD CRAB

DO YOU LIKE A GOOD CULINARY CHALLENGE WITH RECIPES THAT ARE MORE COMPLEX AND A LITTLE BIT FANCY? FROM THE CRUNCHIEST PORK CRACKLING TO THE SOFTEST BEEF CHEEKS, THIS CHAPTER WILL MAKE YOU LOOK LIKE A ROCKSTAR IN THE KITCHEN!

YEE Sang

SERVES 6-8

YEE SANG, OR YU SHENG, MEANS 'RAW DISH', BUT IS ALSO A HOMOPHONE FOR ANOTHER CHINESE WORD MEANING 'AN INCREASE IN ABUNDANCE'. THUS, YEE SANG IS CONSIDERED A SYMBOL OF PROSPERITY AND IS USUALLY ONLY SERVED ON SPECIAL OCCASIONS, ESPECIALLY DURING LUNAR NEW YEAR.

YEE SANG IS A REFRESHING SALAD THAT CONSISTS OF DIFFERENT SHREDDED VEGETABLES AND SLICES OF RAW FISH MIXED WITH SAUCES AND CONDIMENTS, AND IS USUALLY SERVED AS A STARTER TO A CHINESE BANQUET. WHAT MAKES THIS DISH SO SPECIAL IS THE INTERACTION BETWEEN ALL THE DINERS. AS IT'S SERVED, EVERYONE STANDS AROUND THE TABLE WITH CHOPSTICKS AT THE READY. THE HOST ADDS CONDIMENTS AND SAUCES, THEN EVERYONE TOSSES THE INGREDIENTS INTO THE AIR, MAKING WISHES FOR A PROSPEROUS NEW YEAR. IT'S BELIEVED THE HIGHER YOU TOSS, THE GREATER YOUR FORTUNES.

vegetable oil, for deep-frying
½ packet wonton wrappers,
  cut into 1 cm (½ inch) strips
100 g (3½ oz) dried rice
  vermicelli noodles
½ daikon (white radish)
1 cucumber
2 large carrots, peeled
250 g (9 oz) sashimi-grade
  salmon fillet, thinly sliced
1 grapefruit, segmented and
  cut into small bite-sized
  pieces
200 g (7 oz) packet Japanese
  red pickled ginger

SAUCES AND CONDIMENTS
200 ml (7 fl oz) plum sauce
1 tablespoon hoisin sauce
70 g (2½ oz/½ cup) unsalted
  peanuts, toasted and
  roughly chopped
2 tablespoons sesame seeds,
  toasted
2 teaspoons five-spice
  powder
1 teaspoon ground white
  pepper
1 spring onion (scallion),
  thinly sliced
a few wedges of lime

1 Pour the vegetable oil into a medium saucepan until about one-third full, then heat the oil to 180°C (350°F) over medium–high heat. Test to see if the oil is hot enough by dipping a wooden chopstick into the hot oil — if the oil starts steadily bubbling around the chopstick, it's ready. Working in batches, deep-fry the wonton strips until crispy and golden brown. Remove with a slotted spoon and drain on paper towel.

2 Working in batches and using the same hot oil, deep-fry the vermicelli noodles. The noodles will puff up within seconds; remove the crispy noodles with kitchen tongs and drain on paper towel.

3 Using a serrated vegetable peeler, shred the daikon, cucumber and carrots into thin strips. Lightly squeeze the water out of the cucumber strips with both hands, then lay them on paper towel to dry.

4 Arrange the salmon slices in the centre of a large platter. Surround the salmon with the fried wonton strips and crispy noodles, then arrange all the vegetable ingredients, the grapefruit and pickled ginger around the plate like a wheel of fortune.

5 Place all the sauces and condiments in small bowls on the table. Then invite everyone to use their chopsticks to toss the yee sang into the air!

A little BEET of this & a LITTLE BEET of that

BEETROOT. YOU EITHER LOVE OR HATE IT. I USED TO HATE IT, BECAUSE I WAS WOEFULLY MISLED FOR MANY YEARS BY CANNED BEETROOT, WHICH TASTES MUDDY AND INSIPID AND NOTHING LIKE THE FRESH VEGETABLE. THIS RECIPE SHOWCASES THE BEAUTIFUL EARTHY FLAVOUR OF BEETROOT USING SEVERAL TECHNIQUES. THE STRIKING PURPLE-MAROON COLOUR JUST SHOUTS 'EAT ME!'

BEETROOT CHIPS

1 medium beetroot, peeled
olive oil
sea salt flakes

BEETROOT JUS

2 medium beetroots, unpeeled
250 ml (8½ fl oz/1 cup) water
55 g (2 oz/¼ cup) sugar
1 tablespoon lemon juice

ROASTED BEETROOTS

2 medium beetroots, unpeeled
olive oil
sea salt flakes

TORTELLINI

300 g (10½ oz/2 cups) '00' strong flour, plus extra for dusting
100 g (3½ oz) beetroot purée (the remaining beetroot solids from the jus)
1 egg
pinch of salt
50 g (2 oz) blue cheese

100 g (3½ oz) black pudding, removed from sausage casing and finely chopped
small handful of baby beetroot leaves, rinsed and dried
parsley microherb, as garnish

1 Preheat the oven to 160°C (320°F). Line a baking tray with baking paper. To make the beetroot chips, use a mandolin to slice the beetroot as thinly as possible, about 1 mm ($\frac{1}{16}$ inch) thick. Place the beetroot slices on the prepared tray, without overlapping the slices. Lightly drizzle olive oil over the beetroot, then place another baking tray on top to keep the beetroot slices nice and flat while cooking. Bake for 20 minutes, or until the beetroot chips are crispy. Remove the top tray, sprinkle salt over the chips and set aside to cool.

2 Next, cook the 4 beetroots, ready for the beetroot jus and roasted beetroots. Put the 4 unpeeled beetroots in a large saucepan and add enough water to cover them. Put the lid on and bring to the boil, then turn the heat down to medium and simmer until the beetroots are cooked. This can take anywhere between 30 and 40 minutes. Test for doneness by inserting a knife into the thickest part of the beetroot; if the knife goes through easily, it is ready. Pour the hot water out and fill the same pan with cold water. Peel the beetroots by simply rubbing the skins off with both hands (do this in the water so the beetroots won't stain your hands too much). Drain and set aside.

3 To make the beetroot jus, put 2 of the cooked beetroots and the water in a food processor and purée until smooth. Press the purée through a fine sieve set over a saucepan. Keep the beetroot solids in the sieve for later use. Add the sugar and lemon juice to the beetroot juice in the pan and bring to the boil over medium–high heat. Simmer until it reduces by half. Remove from the heat, then strain the jus into a bowl and set aside to cool completely.

4 To make the tortellini, put the flour in a large mixing bowl and make a well in the centre. Add 100 g (3½ oz) of the leftover beetroot purée (keep the rest for serving), the egg and a pinch of salt. Using a fork, stir until everything just comes together. Tip the mixture out onto a lightly floured surface and knead for 2–3 minutes until it forms a smooth dough. Wrap in plastic wrap and rest the dough in the refrigerator for 20 minutes.

5 Cut the dough in half. Start with only one half of the dough and wrap the other half in plastic wrap and put it back in the refrigerator. Use a pasta rolling machine and start from the widest setting. Feed the dough through the machine a few times, adjusting the rollers to the next narrower setting until you reach number four. Roll the dough into a long, flat strip, about 2 mm ($\frac{1}{16}$ inch) thick. Using a pasta trimmer, cut the dough into neat 6 cm (2½ inch) squares.

6 Place ½ teaspoon of blue cheese in the centre of each square. Dab some water along the edges of the pasta, then fold one corner of the pasta over the filling to form a triangle. Press the pasta gently to get rid of any air pockets, and seal the cheese inside. Next pick up the two bottom corners and fold them towards you until they meet; pinch the corners together to make a crown. Place the tortellini on a lightly floured tray. Repeat until all the tortellini are folded. Remove the remaining portion of dough from the refrigerator and repeat the process, to make about 20 tortellini in total. Cover the tortellini with plastic wrap until they are ready to be cooked.

7 To make the roasted beetroot, preheat the oven to 220°C (430°F). Line a baking tray with baking paper. Cut the 2 beetroots into quarters and then halve each quarter. Spread the beetroots on the prepared tray, lightly drizzle with olive oil and sprinkle with sea salt. Bake for 25–30 minutes until the beetroots are nice and crisp on the outside. Remove from the oven and set aside.

8 Meanwhile, heat 2 tablespoons of olive oil in a frying pan and fry the chopped black pudding for 5 minutes, or until blackened and crispy. Remove and drain on paper towel.

9 When it is time to cook the pasta, add a pinch of salt to a pot of water and bring to the boil. Cook the tortellini in batches; the tortellini will float to the surface once they are cooked. Remove with a slotted spoon and place in a mixing bowl. Drizzle with olive oil to stop them from sticking to each other.

10 To serve, brush the beetroot jus around the plate, place a spoonful of beetroot purée in the centre of the plate, then top with roasted beetroot, beetroot tortellini and beetroot chips. Sprinkle the black pudding crumbs all over, then garnish with baby beetroot leaves and microherbs.

Nyonya
DEVIL CURRY

AS THE NAME SUGGESTS, DEVIL CURRY IS ONE HELL OF A CURRY. IT IS SUPER 'I'M SO GOING TO REGRET THIS TOMORROW MORNING' SPICY HOT! THE NUMBER OF CHILLIES USED DETERMINES THE SPICY HEAT LEVEL OF THIS DISH; USE LESS OR SEED THE CHILLIES IF YOU CAN'T HANDLE THE HEAT. THE DEVIL'S CURRY TASTES EVEN BETTER IF YOU LEAVE IT IN THE REFRIGERATOR AND LET THE FLAVOURS DEVELOP OVERNIGHT.

1.5 kg (3 lb 5 oz) free-range whole chicken, cut into bite-sized pieces

2 tablespoons Worcestershire sauce

1 tablespoon lime juice

1 tablespoon sugar

pinch each of salt and ground white pepper

125 ml (4 fl oz/½ cup) vegetable oil

1 red onion, quartered

2 large red chillies, sliced on the diagonal

5 cm (2 inch) piece ginger, grated

125 ml (4 fl oz/½ cup) white vinegar

110 g (3¾ oz/½ cup) sugar

½ teaspoon salt

750 ml (25 fl oz/3 cups) water

200 g (7 oz) cabbage, cut into chunks

100 g (3½ oz) cherry tomatoes

SPICE PASTE

30 g (1 oz) dried red chillies, soaked in hot water for 30 minutes until softened, then drained

100 g (3½ oz) French shallots, peeled

2 cm (¾ inch) piece fresh turmeric, peeled

5 garlic cloves, peeled

1 Put the chicken pieces in a large glass or non-stainless steel bowl. Combine the Worcestershire sauce, lime juice, sugar, salt and white pepper, and pour over the chicken. Stir to combine, then cover and place in the refrigerator to marinate for 30 minutes.

2 To make the spice paste, put all the ingredients into a food processor and process into a fine paste.

3 Heat the vegetable oil in a wok over medium–high heat. Working in batches, fry the chicken for 10 minutes, or until browned. Remove and drain on paper towel. Reheat the oil in the wok, then add the spice paste and fry for about 5 minutes, or until fragrant. Return the chicken pieces to the wok, add the onion, chillies and ginger and stir to mix well.

4 Add the vinegar, sugar, salt and water, then turn the heat down to medium–low and let it simmer for 15 minutes, or until the sauce has reduced by half. Add the cabbage and cherry tomatoes, give it a stir and then simmer for a further 5 minutes before serving.

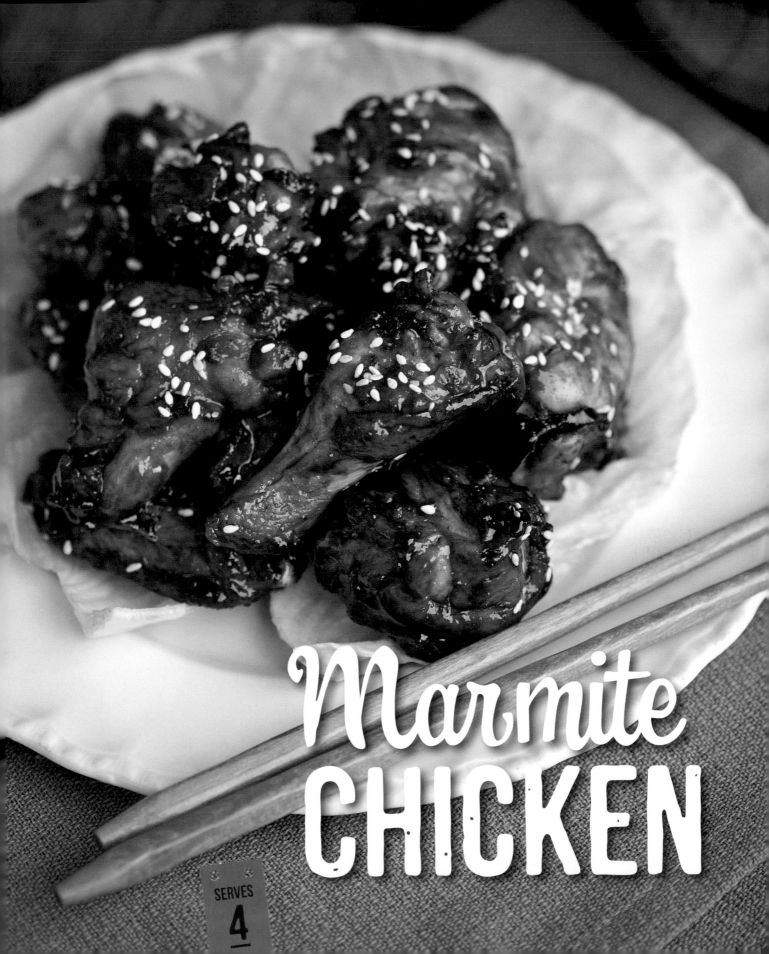

Marmite CHICKEN

SERVES 4

- 500 g (1 lb 2 oz) chicken pieces, such as drumsticks, wings or marylands, cut into bite-sized pieces (or use half a chicken)
- 1 teaspoon light soy sauce, plus
- 1 tablespoon extra for the sauce
- 1 tablespoon oyster sauce
- $\frac{1}{2}$ egg, beaten
- 2 tablespoons cornflour (cornstarch)
- 2 tablespoons rice flour
- vegetable oil, for deep-frying
- 1 tablespoon Marmite yeast extract
- 1 tablespoon honey
- $2\frac{1}{2}$ tablespoons water
- 1 teaspoon dark soy caramel
- pinch of freshly ground black pepper
- pinch of sesame seeds, toasted

1 Put the chicken pieces in a bowl with the teaspoon of light soy sauce, the oyster sauce, beaten egg, cornflour and rice flour. Stir to combine, then place in the refrigerator to marinate for at least 1 hour.

2 Pour the vegetable oil into a large saucepan until about half full, then heat the oil to 180°C (350°F) over medium–high heat. Test to see if the oil is hot enough by dipping a wooden chopstick into the hot oil — if the oil starts steadily bubbling around the chopstick, it's ready. Working in batches, deep-fry the chicken until golden brown. This will take about 10–15 minutes depending on the size of the chicken pieces. Drain on paper towel and set aside.

3 Combine the Marmite, honey, water, dark soy caramel and extra tablespoon of light soy sauce in a bowl, stirring until the Marmite is dissolved. Heat a wok over medium–high heat, pour in the sauce, then add the pepper and continue to stir until the sauce has thickened and reduced to one-third of its original volume. Return the chicken to the wok, and toss everything together until the chicken pieces are evenly coated in the sauce. Transfer to a serving plate and sprinkle with sesame seeds. Serve with steamed rice.

IF YOU ARE A VEGEMITE AND BOVRIL LOVER, THEN YOU WILL LOVE MARMITE CHICKEN. I AM 99.99 PER CENT SURE THAT THIS DISH ORIGINATED FROM MALAYSIA; IT WAS A BIG HIT BACK IN THE EARLY 90S, AND ALMOST EVERY CHINESE RESTAURANT HAD ITS OWN VERSION, WHICH THEY CLAIMED TO BE THE BEST IN TOWN. 'BUT MARMITE AND CHICKEN TOGETHER?', I HEAR YOU SAY! AS PECULIAR AND ABSURD AS IT MAY SOUND, THE NATURAL SAVOURY FLAVOUR OF MARMITE WORKS BEAUTIFULLY WITH SOY SAUCE AND HONEY. YOU WILL JUST HAVE TO GIVE IT A TRY!

Note: You can also use this same recipe for pork ribs or prawns; they both taste just as nice.

Buddha's bowl

CHICKEN AND MARINADE

4 boneless, skinless chicken thighs, cut into 2 cm ($\frac{3}{4}$ inch) cubes

1 teaspoon sugar

1 teaspoon sesame oil

1 teaspoon salt

1 teaspoon Shaoxing rice wine

1 teaspoon cornflour (cornstarch)

SERVES
4

TARO RING

300 g (10$\frac{1}{2}$ oz) taro, peeled and cut into 2 cm ($\frac{3}{4}$ inch) cubes

1 teaspoon sesame oil

3 tablespoons vegetable oil

2 teaspoons sugar

$\frac{1}{2}$ teaspoon five-spice powder

$\frac{1}{2}$ teaspoon salt

pinch of ground white pepper

60 g (2 oz) wheat starch (see note)

1$\frac{1}{2}$ tablespoons hot water

vegetable oil, for deep-frying

100 g (3$\frac{1}{2}$ oz) dried rice vermicelli noodles

FILLING

4 tablespoons vegetable oil

$\frac{1}{2}$ onion, diced

$\frac{1}{2}$ carrot, diced

$\frac{1}{2}$ celery stalk, diced

2 dried shiitake mushrooms, soaked in hot water for 1 hour, stalks discarded, thinly sliced

$\frac{1}{2}$ green capsicum (pepper), diced

6 fresh baby corn, cut into 2 cm ($\frac{3}{4}$ inch) pieces

2 tablespoons oyster sauce

1 teaspoon light soy sauce

1 teaspoon sesame oil

1 teaspoon Shaoxing rice wine

1 teaspoon sugar

pinch of salt

small handful of cashew nuts, toasted

THIS DISH IS SO CALLED BECAUSE OF ITS RESEMBLANCE TO THE BOWL USED BY BUDDHIST MONKS TO COLLECT ALMS FROM THEIR COMMUNITY. HERE THE 'BOWL' IS A RING OF DEEP-FRIED TARO, WHICH IS FILLED WITH STIR-FRIED CHICKEN AND VEGETABLES. MY FAVOURITE PART IS DEFINITELY THE TARO RING: THE INSIDE IS SOFT AND FLUFFY LIKE POTATO MASH, AND THE OUTSIDE IS GOLDEN AND CRISPY. DUE TO GETTING 'LOST IN TRANSLATION' MANY RECIPES REFER TO THIS AS A YAM RING. ALTHOUGH THESE TWO ROOT VEGETABLES ARE SIMILAR, THE RING IS MADE FROM TARO, NOT YAM. TARO USUALLY HAS A WHITE FLESH WITH SOME PURPLISH FIBROUS SPECKS THROUGHOUT – MAKE SURE YOU GET THE RIGHT INGREDIENT OR IT WON'T WORK.

1 Put the chicken in a mixing bowl. Combine the marinade ingredients and pour over the chicken. Cover and place in the refrigerator to marinate for 30 minutes.

2 To prepare the taro ring, set a steamer over boiling water and steam the taro cubes for 25–30 minutes until soft. Mash the taro through a sieve into a bowl, then mix in the sesame oil, vegetable oil, sugar, five-spice, salt and white pepper. Combine the wheat starch and hot water in another bowl, then knead into a small ball of dough. Add the dough to the mashed taro and knead until it becomes elastic and pliable.

3 Transfer the dough to a lightly oiled surface and roll the dough out into a long thick strip, about 40 cm (16 inches) in length. Lightly oil the inside of a round cake tin or a medium saucepan to use as a guide, then carefully wrap the strip of dough inside the tin to form a hollow ring, about 2 cm ($\frac{3}{4}$ inch) thick, 6–8 cm ($2\frac{1}{2}$–$3\frac{1}{4}$ inches) high and about 15 cm (6 inches) in diameter. Gently remove the taro ring and set aside on a tray.

4 Pour the vegetable oil into a wok until about one-third full (the taro ring needs to be at least half submerged in oil), then heat the oil to 180°C (350°F) over medium–high heat. Test to see if the oil is hot enough by dipping a wooden chopstick into the hot oil — if the oil starts steadily bubbling around

the chopstick, it's ready. Working in two batches, drop a handful of vermicelli into the hot oil — the noodles will puff up within seconds. Remove and drain on paper towel.

5 Using 2 spatulas, carefully lift the taro ring and lower it into the hot oil. Deep-fry for 5 minutes, or until golden brown, then carefully turn it over and cook for a further 5 minutes. To make sure the taro ring is cooking evenly, use a metal spoon to ladle hot oil over the ring while it is deep-frying. Remove and drain on paper towel.

6 To make the filling, heat 2 tablespoons of the vegetable oil in a wok over high heat. Add the chicken and stir-fry for 3 minutes until cooked, then remove and set aside. Wipe the wok with paper towel. Reheat the wok with the remaining 2 tablespoons of vegetable oil, then add the onion, carrot and celery and stir-fry for about 1 minute, or until the onion is translucent and fragrant. Add the mushroom, capsicum and baby corn and stir-fry for another 2 minutes. Add the oyster sauce, soy sauce, sesame oil and rice wine. Season with sugar and salt, give it a quick stir, then toss the chicken back into the wok and mix well. Remove from the heat.

7 Spread the puffed crispy noodles on a large serving plate. Place the taro ring on top and fill the centre with the chicken and vegetables. Sprinkle sparingly with cashews.

Note: Wheat starch, or tung meen fun in Chinese, must not be mistaken with wheat flour. Wheat starch is a non-glutinous flour and is usually used to make dim sum, resulting in a translucent skin and chewy texture. Wheat starch can be found in Asian grocers, or can be substituted with cornflour (cornstarch), but the texture won't be exactly the same.

Roast duck & LYCHEE red curry

2 tablespoons vegetable oil

300 ml (10 fl oz) tinned coconut cream

150 g (5 oz) tinned lychees, drained, reserving 250 ml (8½ fl oz/1 cup) of the syrup

500 g (1 lb 2 oz) roast duck (page 32), or use a store-bought duck, chopped into bite-sized pieces

100 g (3½ oz) cherry tomatoes

4 baby corn, cut into small pieces

10 snow peas (mangetout)

fish sauce, to taste

squeeze of lime juice

2 kaffir lime leaves, rolled and thinly sliced

RED CURRY PASTE

4 dried red chillies, soaked in hot water for 30 minutes, then drained

8 large red chillies (seeded if preferred)

4 French shallots, peeled

2 lemongrass stalks, white parts only

4 garlic cloves, peeled

2 tablespoons ground coriander seeds

5 cm (2 inch) piece galangal, peeled and sliced

10 g (½ oz) belachan (dried shrimp paste), toasted

2 tablespoons grated palm sugar (jaggery)

5 candlenuts, roasted (see note page 272)

pinch of ground white pepper

2 tablespoons fish sauce

125 ml (4 fl oz/½ cup) tinned coconut milk

1 To make the red curry paste, put all the ingredients in a food processor and process to form a fine paste.

2 Heat the vegetable oil in a large saucepan over medium–high heat and fry the curry paste for 5 minutes, or until fragrant. Add the coconut cream and reserved lychee syrup and bring to the boil, then add the duck meat and simmer for 10 minutes. Add the lychees, cherry tomatoes, baby corn and snow peas, cover and simmer for a further 5 minutes.

3 Season the curry with fish sauce and a squeeze of lime juice, to taste. Transfer the curry to a large serving bowl and garnish with lime leaves. Serve with steamed rice.

SYDNEY IS BLESSED WITH A PLETHORA OF THAI RESTAURANTS — THERE SEEMS TO BE A THAI RESTAURANT ON EVERY STREET CORNER IN EVERY SUBURB. I'VE BEEN TO THAILAND NUMEROUS TIMES AND I THINK THE THAI FOOD IN SYDNEY IS ALMOST JUST AS GOOD! THIS ROAST DUCK CURRY IS ONE OF MY FAVOURITE THAI DISHES. I LOVE HOW THE SWEET LYCHEES WORK SO WELL WITH THE HEAT OF THE CURRY AND THE GAMEY ROAST DUCK. THE RED CURRY PASTE IS THE SOUL OF THIS DISH, SO IT IS IMPORTANT TO TAKE YOUR TIME AND COOK IT WITH LOVE. ONCE YOU'VE GOT THE PASTE RIGHT, THE REST IS A WALK IN THE PARK.

SERVES
4

Perfect ROAST PORK BELLY in APPLE CIDER

WHAT MAKES THE PERFECT ROAST PORK BELLY? IN MY OPINION IT IS A SLOW-BRAISED SUCCULENT TENDER BELLY THAT SIMPLY MELTS IN THE MOUTH, AND IT HAS THAT GOLDEN EARTH-SHATTERING CRUNCHY CRACKLING ON TOP. WELL ... ACTUALLY, IT'S ALL ABOUT THE CRACKLING! HERE ARE A FEW HANDY TIPS TO ACHIEVE THAT PERFECT CRACKLING. FIRSTLY, WHEN SCORING THE SKIN, MAKE SURE THE SCORE LINES ARE CUT ALL THE WAY TO THE EDGES SO THE FAT CAN BE RENDERED OUT. SECONDLY, MAKE SURE THE RIND IS AS DRY AS POSSIBLE, LEAVE IT IN THE REFRIGERATOR OVERNIGHT TO HELP DEHYDRATE THE SKIN FURTHER. THIRDLY, SALT – IT HELPS TO DRAW MOISTURE OUT OF THE SKIN WHEN ROASTING. LASTLY, IF THE PORK BELLY COMES IN UNEVEN THICKNESS, RAISE THE THINNER PART BY PUTTING SOME VEGETABLES OFF-CUTS UNDERNEATH UNTIL YOU HAVE A FLAT SURFACE.

1.8 kg (4 lb) pork belly, with skin on
65 g (2¼ oz) rock salt or sea salt flakes
olive oil, to drizzle
3 carrots, cut into chunks
2 celery stalks, cut into chunks
2 apples, cut into chunks
365 ml (13 fl oz) bottle apple cider

375 ml (13 fl oz/1½ cups) chicken stock
1 tablespoon fennel seeds
2 bay leaves
3 sprigs thyme
2 tablespoons cornflour (cornstarch), mixed with 4 tablespoons water
20 g (¾ oz) chilled butter, cut into cubes
salt and pepper

APPLE GRATIN
3 Granny Smith apples
2 tablespoons apple cider vinegar
2 tablespoons sugar
3 sprigs thyme, leaves picked

ROAST CARROTS
1 knob of butter
1 bunch Dutch (baby) carrots

SERVES
6-8

1 Preheat the oven to 250°C (500°F). Move the wire rack in the oven to the level closest to the top element.

2 To clean the pork belly, scrape the skin with the blade of a knife to remove any hair, then pat dry all over with paper towel. Score the skin crosswise in vertical lines about 2–3 cm ($\frac{3}{4}$–$1\frac{1}{4}$ inches) apart, then flip the pork belly over and do the same on the meat side, cutting about 1 cm ($\frac{1}{2}$ inch) deep.

3 Bring a kettle to the boil, then pour the hot water over the skin to scald it. The skin will tighten and the score lines will widen, revealing the fat underneath. Pat with paper towel until completely dry, then place on a baking tray. For the best results and a crunchier crackling, you can dehydrate the pork by leaving it uncovered in the refrigerator overnight. If not, rub salt on the skin and into the score lines, then drizzle with olive oil.

4 Transfer the tray to the top rack in the oven and grill (broil) the pork for about 45 minutes until the skin evenly crackles and is blisteringly crunchy. Make sure the kitchen is well ventilated, as it will get very smoky because of the burning fat on the tray. Take the tray out of the oven every 10 minutes or so to tip the rendered fat out into a bowl; discard it.

5 Once ready, take the pork out of the oven, reduce the oven to 150°C (300°F) and move the wire rack to the middle of the oven. Transfer the pork to a baking dish and surround it with the carrots, celery and apples. Open the bottle of apple cider and carefully pour it into the dish without wetting the pork skin. Then top it up with chicken stock, using only enough to cover the meat and not the skin. Add the fennel seeds and bay leaves to the stock. Place the dish on the middle rack in the oven and roast the pork for 3 hours.

6 Start preparing the apple gratin and roast carrots and get them into the oven for the last hour of cooking. For the gratin, use a mandolin to thinly slice the apples into a bowl. Add the apple cider vinegar, sugar and thyme leaves, and toss to mix well. Spread the mixture evenly in a small rectangular baking dish.

7 For the roast carrots, melt the butter in a frying pan and cook the carrots for about 5 minutes, or until caramelised on the outside, then transfer to a small baking dish. Place both the apple and carrot dishes on the wire rack in the oven below the pork and roast for 1 hour, or until the pork is ready.

8 Remove all the dishes from the oven. Let the pork rest in the liquid for 15 minutes before transferring it onto a chopping board. Strain the liquid in the baking dish into a saucepan to make a gravy, and keep the braised vegetables and apples to make a purée. To make the purée, put the braised vegetables, apples and 3 tablespoons of the braising stock into a food processor and process until smooth. Season with salt and pepper and set aside. To make the gravy, put the remaining braising stock and thyme sprigs into a saucepan. Bring to the boil, then reduce the liquid until there is only 250 ml ($8\frac{1}{2}$ fl oz/1 cup) of liquid left. Stir in the cornflour and water mixture, then whisk in the butter a bit at a time until the gravy thickens. Season with salt and pepper, then strain through a fine sieve into a jug.

9 To serve, place a few spoonfuls of purée on each plate, and then top with some pork belly and roasted carrots. Cut the apple gratin into smaller portions and serve it on the side. Pour over the gravy.

SOME OF THE BEST MEALS I'VE SHARED WITH FRIENDS ARE THOSE EATEN WITHOUT CUTLERY. YOU CAN SHRED THE MEAT BEFOREHAND AND SERVE IT IN LETTUCE CUPS WITH ACAR AWAK SALAD ON THE SIDE. OR MAKE IT A D.I.Y. AFFAIR AND JUST PLONK THE WHOLE HUNK OF PORK SHOULDER IN THE MIDDLE OF THE TABLE WITH ENOUGH TONGS AND FORKS, SO EVERYONE CAN DIG IN AND PULL OFF AS MUCH OF THE TENDER PORK MEAT AS THEY LIKE. FRIENDS, LAUGHTER, BEER, JUICY PORK — WHAT MORE COULD YOU WANT?

PULLED PORK
& *Acar Awak*
LETTUCE WRAP

3–4 kg (6 lb 9 oz–8 lb 12 oz)
pork shoulder or
forequarter
130 g (4½ oz/½ cup) cooking or
table salt
110 g (3¾ oz/½ cup) sugar
110 g (3¾ oz/½ cup firmly
packed) light brown sugar
Acar awak (page 72)
1 iceberg lettuce, leaves
separated and trimmed
into individual cups
(see note)

MARINADE

1 large onion, finely chopped
3 garlic cloves, finely chopped
4 tablespoons apple cider
vinegar
125 ml (4 fl oz/½ cup) smoked
barbecue sauce
2 tablespoons smoked
paprika
45 g (1½ oz/¼ cup lightly
packed) light brown sugar
2 tablespoons
Worcestershire sauce
1 tablespoon cayenne pepper

1 Place the pork shoulder in a large roasting tin; remove the skin and trim off any excess fat. Mix together the salt, sugar and brown sugar in a bowl, then rub the mixture into the pork. Cover and place in the refrigerator to marinate for at least 6 hours, or ideally overnight.

2 Preheat the oven to 150°C (300°F). Remove the pork from the refrigerator, discard any juices in the tin and brush off any salt residue on the pork. Leave the pork to come to room temperature while you prepare the sauce.

3 Combine all the marinade ingredients in a mixing bowl, stir well, then pour the marinade all over the pork and give it a good rub to make sure it is well coated.

4 Put the pork in the oven and cook for 5 hours, basting with the rendered fat and pan juices every hour. The pork should be tender and yielding, and you should be easily able to pull the meat off the shoulder using a fork.

5 Once ready, remove the roasting tin from the oven and let the pork rest in the sauce until it is cool enough to handle. With a fork in each hand, pull the shoulder apart into shredded meat and let it soak up all the beautiful sauce in the tin.

6 To serve, place a generous pile of pulled pork meat in a lettuce cup, then top with spicy acar awak.

Note: I find the easiest way to split an iceberg lettuce into individual leaves is to remove the stalk first, then bounce the lettuce on a work bench to loosen the leaves — you are then be able to separate the leaves easily.

SERVES
8
TO
12

Twice-cooked
PORK BELLY with APPLE
& CABBAGE SLAW

EVERYONE SHOULD LEARN HOW TO MAKE A MASTERSTOCK. A MASTERSTOCK IS A CHINESE STOCK USED FOR POACHING AND BRAISING, OR IT CAN BE REDUCED DOWN INTO AN AROMATIC SAUCE. AS LONG AS IT IS STORED IN THE FREEZER, IT WILL LAST FOR A VERY LONG TIME AND CAN BE REUSED OVER AND OVER AGAIN. THE MORE PROTEINS COOKED IN THE STOCK, THE BETTER THE FLAVOUR BECOMES. IN THIS RECIPE, THE MASTERSTOCK IS USED FOR SLOW-BRAISING THE PORK BELLY, AND IS THEN USED TO MAKE THE CHILLI CARAMEL SAUCE.

1 kg (2 lb 3 oz) pork belly, with
    skin off
240 g (8½ oz/2 cups) tapioca
    starch
1 tablespoon five-spice powder
1 teaspoon salt
vegetable oil, for
    deep-frying

CHINESE MASTERSTOCK

3 litres (102 fl oz) water
250 ml (8½ fl oz/1 cup) light soy
    sauce
3 tablespoons dark soy caramel
250 ml (8½ fl oz/1 cup) Shaoxing
    rice wine
200 g (7 oz) Chinese yellow rock
    sugar (see note)
5 garlic cloves, sliced
5 spring onions (scallions),
    white part only
1 cassia bark or cinnamon stick
1 teaspoon cloves
1 teaspoon coriander seeds
1 teaspoon Sichuan
    peppercorns
5 star anise
3 pieces dried mandarin peel

CHILLI CARAMEL SAUCE

500 ml (17 fl oz/2 cups)
    masterstock
    (from braising the pork belly)
3 bird's eye chillies, finely
    chopped
115 g (4 oz/½ cup) caster
    (superfine) sugar
125 ml (4 fl oz/½ cup) fish sauce
3 tablespoons light soy sauce
2 garlic cloves, finely chopped

APPLE AND CABBAGE SLAW

1 Granny Smith apple,
    julienned into matchsticks
100 g (3½ oz) cabbage, finely
    shredded
juice of ½ lemon

1 To make the masterstock, fill a large pot with the water, then add all the stock ingredients. Stir and then bring to the boil over high heat. Once boiling, reduce the heat to medium–low and simmer for 30 minutes. Turn the heat off and allow the stock to cool. Strain, discarding the solids. Use immediately or store in the refrigerator.

2 Preheat the oven to 150°C (300°F). Place the pork belly in a roasting tin, then pour in enough masterstock to fully cover the pork. Cover the stock with a sheet of baking paper as a cartouche, pressing down so it touches the surface of the stock. Transfer to the oven and braise for 4 hours.

3 Remove the tin from the oven and let the pork rest in the stock until cool, then transfer the pork to a plate or tray. Cover with plastic wrap and refrigerate. Reserve the stock for the sauce.

4 To make the chilli caramel sauce, put all the ingredients in a saucepan over medium–high heat and bring to the boil. Reduce the heat to medium–low and simmer until the sauce has thickened and reduced to a quarter of its original amount. Strain, then set aside to cool.

5 To make the slaw, place the apple and cabbage in a mixing bowl. Squeeze the lemon juice over, then toss to mix well. Cover with plastic wrap and transfer to the refrigerator.

6 Cut the pork belly into 5 cm (2 inch) cubes. Mix the tapioca starch, five-spice and salt in a mixing bowl. Roll the pork pieces in the starch until evenly coated, then dust off any excess.

7 Pour the vegetable oil into a large saucepan until about half full, then heat the oil to 170°C (340°F) over medium–high heat. Test to see if the oil is hot enough by dipping a wooden chopstick into the hot oil — if the oil starts bubbling around the chopstick, it's ready. Working in batches, deep-fry the pork belly for 5–7 minutes until dark golden brown. Remove and drain on paper towel.

8 Stack the pork belly high in a serving bowl, drizzle the chilli caramel sauce over the pork, then top with some apple and cabbage slaw.

Note: Chinese yellow rock sugar, sometimes called rock candy, is not quite as sweet as normal granulated sugar and is a key ingredient in Chinese masterstock. It can be found in Asian grocers.

AUSSIE DAMPER *Wagyu* BURGER

EVERYONE SHOULD HAVE A GOOD BURGER RECIPE IN THEIR COOKING REPERTOIRE. I LOVE A GOOD OLE AUSSIE BURGER WITH A THICK, JUICY BEEF PATTIE SANDWICHED BETWEEN A SOFT CRUMBLY DAMPER ROLL. AND DON'T FORGET THE BEETROOT; IT'S NOT AN AUSSIE BURGER WITHOUT IT! THIS IS A RECIPE THAT I LIKE TO COOK IN THE OUTDOORS WITH NOTHING BUT A CAMPFIRE. I RECKON THE DAMPER ROLL CAN BE LISTED AS ONE OF THE SEVEN WONDERS OF THE CULINARY WORLD, AS IT DOESN'T NEED YEAST OR BAKING POWDER TO RISE — ALL IT NEEDS IS A BOTTLE OF BEER! HOW TRUE-BLUE AUSSIE IS THAT?

DAMPER BUNS

300 g (10½ oz/2 cups) self-
   raising flour, plus extra
   for dusting
60 g (2 oz) butter, melted
1 teaspoon salt
150 ml (5 fl oz) beer
2 tablespoons milk,
   for brushing

WAGYU BEEF PATTIES

600 g (1 lb 5 oz) minced
   (ground) wagyu beef
   (or use very good quality
   minced beef)
1 onion, finely diced
1 teaspoon ground cumin
   seeds
1 teaspoon finely chopped
   rosemary
110 g (3¾ oz/1 cup) dry
   breadcrumbs
1 egg, lightly beaten
2 tablespoons smoked
   barbecue sauce
   (see note)
pinch of salt and freshly
   ground black pepper

1 whole large beetroot,
   with skin on
300 g (10½ oz) frozen
   shoestring fries
vegetable oil, for deep-
   frying
sea salt flakes
8 slices cheddar cheese
4 eggs
1 cos (romaine) lettuce,
   stalk removed, washed
   and leaves picked
Chilli onion jam
   (page 275)

1 Preheat the oven to 200°C (400°F). Lightly dust a baking tray with flour. To make the damper buns, put all the ingredients, except the milk, in a bowl. Use a fork to mix everything together until it forms a rough dough, then transfer the dough to a floured surface and knead for 5 minutes, or until the dough is smooth. If the dough is a bit wet, add a little more flour until it no longer sticks to your hands. Roll the dough into a log, then divide it into 4 equal portions. Roll each portion into a small ball, then use your palms to flatten the dough into a disc, about 2.5 cm (1 inch) thick. Place the dough discs on the prepared tray. With a sharp knife, score a cross on each, then brush the top with milk. Bake for 20 minutes, then reduce the heat to 180°C (350°F) and bake for a further 15 minutes, or until the buns are golden brown.

2 To make the beef patties, put all the ingredients in a large bowl, and use your hands to mix everything together until well combined. Take 180 g (6½ oz) of the mixture, roll it into a ball, then flatten slightly. Repeat to make 4 beef patties in total. Cover and refrigerate for 1 hour before cooking.

3 Cook the beetroot in a pot of boiling water for 1 hour, or until tender. Drop the beetroot into cold water to cool, then peel the skin off and thinly slice the beetroot. Set aside.

4 For the shoestring fries, pour the oil into a medium saucepan until about half full, then heat the oil to 180°C (350°F) over medium–high heat. Test to see if the oil is hot enough by dipping a wooden chopstick into the hot oil — if the oil starts steadily bubbling around the chopstick, it's ready. Working in batches, take a handful of the frozen fries and carefully drop them into the hot oil; fry until golden brown. Remove and drain on paper towel, then sprinkle with salt.

5 Preheat the barbecue to medium–high. Use a spatula to flatten the patties slightly, then cook for 5 minutes on each side. Place 2 slices of cheese on each pattie, close the lid and let the cheese melt for a minute or so. Fry the eggs, sunny side up.

6 To assemble the burgers, cut the damper buns in half, spread the cut halves with some butter and toast them on the barbecue, cut sides down. Place the buns on a serving plate, put some lettuce on the bottom bun, top with a beef pattie, a spoonful of chilli onion jam, 2 slices of beetroot and finally top with a fried egg. Serve with the fries on the side.

Note: Use a good-quality smoked barbecue sauce, such as Masterfoods, Jack Daniels or HP, as it adds a nice depth of smoky flavour to the burger. You can find bottles of smoked barbecue sauce in major supermarkets or fine food stores.

Beef Rendang

SERVES
4-6

IF YOU LOVE CURRIES BUT CAN'T HANDLE THE SPICINESS, THEN THIS IS THE CURRY FOR YOU. RENDANG IS A DRY MEAT CURRY THAT ORIGINATES FROM INDONESIA, BUT IS EQUALLY POPULAR IN MALAYSIA, SINGAPORE AND OTHER SOUTHEAST ASIAN COUNTRIES. A GOOD RENDANG SHOULD BE COOKED SLOWLY, THE MEAT GENTLY SIMMERING IN THE RICH SPICE PASTE AND COCONUT MILK UNTIL ALMOST ALL THE LIQUID HAS EVAPORATED AND THE BEEF IS MELTINGLY TENDER.

1 tablespoon coriander seeds

1 teaspoon fennel seeds

1 teaspoon black peppercorns

3 tablespoons vegetable oil

1.5 kg (3 lb 5 oz) topside or chuck steak, cut into 3 cm (1¼ inch) cubes

3 lemongrass stalks, white part only, bruised with a pestle

3 kaffir lime leaves, plus 1 extra, rolled and thinly sliced

540 ml (18 fl oz) tinned coconut milk

250 ml (8½ fl oz/1 cup) water

1 tablespoon salt, or to taste

2 tablespoons sugar, or to taste

90 g (3 oz/1 cup) desiccated coconut

SPICE PASTE

10 g (½ oz) dried red chillies (about 20), soaked in hot water for 30 minutes until softened, then drained

130 g (4¼ oz) French shallots (about 12 small shallots), peeled

4 cm (1½ inch) piece galangal, peeled

4 cm (1½ inch) piece ginger, peeled

2 cm (¾ inch) piece turmeric, peeled (or 1 tablespoon ground turmeric)

1 Toast the coriander seeds, fennel seeds and black peppercorns in a dry frying pan over low heat. Once the fennel seeds start making popping sounds, transfer the toasted spices into a mortar and pestle or a spice grinder, and grind into a fine powder. Set aside.

2 To make the spice paste, put all the ingredients into a food processor and process into a fine paste.

3 Heat the vegetable oil in large saucepan over medium–low heat, add the spice paste and fry gently for 8–10 minutes until fragrant and darker red in colour. Add the beef, lemongrass, 3 whole kaffir lime leaves and ground spices, stirring to mix well. Cook for about 3 minutes until the beef is lightly cooked, then add the coconut milk and water, stir to combine, then turn the heat down to a simmer. Cook, uncovered, for 1½ hours until the meat is tender and the sauce is thick. Season with salt and sugar, to taste.

4 Meanwhile, heat a dry frying pan over low heat. Add the desiccated coconut and toast until golden, stirring constantly so the coconut doesn't burn (take care it doesn't burn or it will have an unpleasant flavour). Set aside to cool, then put in a food processor and pulse a few times until the coconut becomes fine crumbs.

5 Add the toasted coconut to the beef, stirring frequently over low heat for about 15 minutes, or until the coconut releases its oil and is absorbed by the meat. Garnish with the sliced kaffir lime leaf and serve with steamed rice.

BEEF *cheeks* BOURGUIGNON *with* CAULIFLOWER & LEEK PURÉE

BEEF CHEEK IS THE FACIAL MUSCLE OF A COW, AND IF YOU CONSIDER THAT A COW SPENDS THE WHOLE DAY GRAZING, IT'S NO SURPRISE THAT THE CHEEK IS PRETTY TOUGH. IN THE PAST, BEEF CHEEK WAS CONSIDERED A CHEAP CUT, AND IT EVENTUALLY BECAME OBSOLETE. BUT FASHIONS CHANGE AND THE CHEEK HAS MADE A CULINARY COMEBACK; IT'S NOW CONSIDERED QUITE A LUXURY CUT OF MEAT AND OCCASIONALLY CAN BE FOUND ON THE MENUS OF FINE-DINING RESTAURANTS.

SERVES

4

2 large beef cheeks (1.2 kg/
    2 lb 10 oz), halved (see note)
5 sprigs thyme
2 fresh bay leaves
500 ml (17 fl oz/2 cups)
    Pedro Ximenez sherry
    (also known as PX)
500 ml (17 fl oz/2 cups) red
    wine
75 g (2½ oz/½ cup) plain
    (all-purpose) flour,
    for dusting

6 tablespoons olive oil
2 carrots, diced
1 celery stalk, diced
½ leek, white part only, diced
    (see note)
1 large brown onion, diced
500 ml (17 fl oz/2 cups) veal
    or beef stock
salt and pepper
50 g (2 oz) chilled butter,
    cubed

CAULIFLOWER AND LEEK PURÉE

½ head cauliflower, cut into
    small florets
250 ml (8½ fl oz/1 cup) full-
    cream milk
70 g (2½ oz) butter, cubed
½ leek, white part only,
    thinly sliced
salt and pepper

1 Trim any fat and sinews off the beef cheeks and put them in a large deep non-metallic bowl. Add the thyme sprigs and bay leaves, then pour the PX and red wine into the bowl. Cover with plastic wrap and place in the refrigerator to marinate for 4 hours. Turn the beef every hour.

2 Reserving the marinade, remove the beef and pat dry thoroughly. Dredge the beef with flour and shake off the excess, then set aside.

3 In a heavy-based casserole dish, heat 4 tablespoons of the olive oil over medium–high heat, then add the beef cheeks and brown for a few minutes until lightly coloured all over. Remove from the dish and set aside.

4 Add the remaining 2 tablespoons of olive oil to the dish and cook the carrot, celery, leek and onion for 3 minutes, or until the vegetables are caramelised and the onion is soft and translucent. Return the beef cheeks to the dish and pour in the reserved marinade and enough stock to cover the meat. Stir and scrape the base of the dish to deglaze all the caramelised tasty bits. Reduce the heat to low, then cover and cook

for 4 hours, or until the cheeks are meltingly tender but still holding their shape. Season with salt and pepper.

5 Meanwhile, to make the purée, put the cauliflower and milk in a saucepan over low heat and cook for 20–25 minutes until softened. Add a tablespoon of the butter to a frying pan over medium heat and sauté the leek until softened.

6 Transfer the cooked cauliflower and leek to a food processor. Add the remaining butter and process until smooth. Press the purée through a fine sieve into a bowl, then set aside and keep warm. Season with salt and pepper, to taste.

7 To make a jus, strain 500 ml (17 fl oz/ 2 cups) of the braising stock through a fine sieve into a saucepan. Reduce the stock over high heat until glaze-like. Whisk the butter into the sauce a few cubes at a time, stirring until fully emulsified before adding the next cubes of butter.

8 To serve, place a big dollop of cauliflower and leek purée on each plate, then top with a beef cheek and drizzle with the jus.

Note: Beef cheeks can be hard to come by — not many butcher shops stock them and they don't come cheap, so it's best to go to a gourmet butcher or ask your butcher to order them in for you.

OSSO BUCCO MEANS 'BONE WITH A HOLE', AND THIS MILANESE SPECIALTY HAS BECOME ONE OF MY FAVOURITE DISHES TO COOK FOR A NO-FUSS DINNER WITH FRIENDS, WHEN I'D RATHER BE CHATTING WITH MY GUESTS THAN SLAVING OVER A HOT STOVE. SERVE IT WITH SOFT POLENTA TO SOAK UP ALL THE SAUCE. COUSCOUS OR A SIMPLE MASH WORKS BEAUTIFULLY TOO.

Osso bucco
WITH SOFT POLENTA
& corn

4 large veal osso bucco
salt and pepper
75 g (2½ oz/½ cup) plain
(all-purpose) flour,
for dusting
4 tablespoons olive oil
50 g (2 oz) pancetta, cut
into strips
1 onion, finely chopped
2 carrots, diced
1 celery stalk, diced
2 garlic cloves, crushed

500 ml (17 fl oz/2 cups)
beef stock
400 g (14 oz) tinned
crushed tomatoes
about 375 ml (13 fl oz/
1½ cups) white wine
2 bay leaves
3 thyme sprigs
2 corn cobs
40 g (1½ oz) butter

SOFT POLENTA
500 ml (17 fl oz/2 cups)
water
500 ml (17 fl oz/2 cups)
vegetable stock
150 g (5 oz/1 cup) polenta
100 g (3½ oz) butter
250 ml (8½ fl oz/1 cup)
thickened (whipping)
cream (35% fat)
50 g (2 oz/½ cup) grated
parmesan cheese

1 Season the osso bucco with salt and pepper, dust with flour, then shake off any excess. Heat the olive oil in a large pot over medium heat, add the osso bucco and sear on both sides for 3 minutes on each side, or until browned. Remove and set aside.

2 Using the same pot, add the pancetta and cook for 2 minutes, then add the onion, carrot, celery and garlic and sauté for 5 minutes, or until the onion is soft and translucent. Pour in the beef stock to deglaze the pot, then return the osso bucco to the pot. Add the tomatoes, then pour in the white wine until the osso bucco are fully submerged (you'll need about half a bottle). Add the bay leaves and thyme sprigs, turn the heat down to low and simmer for 2 hours.

3 Put the corn cobs in a pot of water and bring to the boil. Cook for 10 minutes, then drain. Cut the kernels off the cobs and set aside.

4 Make the polenta when there is 30 minutes left before the osso bucco is ready. Pour the water and vegetable stock into a saucepan and bring to the boil. Sprinkle the polenta into the pan, stirring continuously to stop the polenta from clumping. Turn the heat down and cook the polenta for 30 minutes until it is soft like mashed potato. Add the butter, cream and parmesan, and stir well until smooth. Mix half of the corn kernels into the polenta.

5 Heat the butter in a small frying pan over medium heat, add the remaining corn kernels and cook for 3 minutes until lightly brown on the edges.

6 To serve, place a ladleful of polenta on each plate, top with the osso bucco and a few spoonfuls of the fried corn kernels.

Ribs
YOUR HEART OUT

2 racks of American-style pork ribs
2 carrots, diced
1 celery stalk, diced
1 brown onion, diced
1 tablespoon fennel seeds
1 litre (34 fl oz/4 cups) vegetable stock
water

MARINADE
125 ml (4 fl oz/½ cup) tomato sauce (ketchup)
125 ml (4 fl oz/½ cup) smoked barbecue sauce
3 tablespoons apple cider vinegar
3 tablespoons bourbon whiskey
1 teaspoon cayenne pepper
1 teaspoon smoked paprika
3 garlic cloves, finely chopped
2 French shallots, finely chopped
1 tablespoon sugar
pinch of salt

1 Preheat the oven to 150°C (300°F). Put the ribs in a roasting tin with the carrots, celery, onion and fennel seeds. Pour the vegetable stock into the tin and add enough water until the ribs are fully covered. Place a piece of baking paper over the top of the ribs, transfer to the oven and braise for 4 hours. Remove the tin from the oven, set aside and let the ribs rest in the stock until completely cool. Take the ribs out and put them on a plate or tray, then cover and chill in the refrigerator for 1 hour. Reserve the stock for other use.

2 Increase the oven to 220°C (430°F). Combine all the ingredients for the marinade in a bowl. Rub 250 ml (8½ fl oz/1 cup) of the marinade all over the ribs, then place them on a baking tray lined with baking paper. Place the tray on the top rack in the oven and grill (broil) the ribs for 30 minutes, or until nicely caramelised. While the ribs are cooking, regularly baste them on both sides with the leftover marinade. Once ready, let them rest on the tray for 10 minutes, brush with more marinade, then cut them up into single or double rib portions. Make sure to have plenty of paper towels for sticky fingers.

YOU MAY HAVE NOTICED FROM SOME OF THE RECIPES IN THIS BOOK THAT I DO HAVE A SOFT SPOT FOR SOUTHERN AMERICAN FOOD — CREOLE, SOUL FOOD, CAJUN, TEX MEX, YOU NAME IT. THE RIBS ARE TWICE COOKED, SOUTHERN STYLE: BRAISED UNTIL THE MEAT IS FALL-OFF-THE-BONE TENDER THEN GRILLED IN THE OVEN TO GET A NICE CARAMELISATION GOING. BUT BE PREPARED FOR STICKY FINGERS; THIS IS CAVEMAN (CAVEPERSON!?) FOOD AT ITS CARNAL BEST.

SERVES
4

I'M A RELATIVE LATECOMER TO THE JOY THAT IS LAMB. IT WAS OFTEN HARD TO GET LAMB MEAT IN MALAYSIA, SO WE ATE A LOT OF GOAT (ALSO KNOWN AS MUTTON IN MALAYSIA). FOR SOME REASON, I ALWAYS THOUGHT GOAT AND LAMB WERE QUITE SIMILAR, WITH THAT STRONG GAMEY FLAVOR, AND SO I TENDED TO AVOID THEM BOTH. OH, HOW WRONG WAS I. I'M NOW A CONVERTED LAMB LOVER AND SIMPLY CAN'T GET ENOUGH OF IT. AND FUNNILY ENOUGH, I EVEN LOVE EATING GOAT MEAT! I MUST BE BAHHHHHH-ING MAD!

Slow-roast LAMB SHOULDER with ROSEMARY & PRESERVED LEMON

2.5 kg (5 lb 8 oz) lamb shoulder, deboned

2 teaspoons sea salt flakes, plus extra to taste

1 teaspoon freshly ground black pepper

3 garlic cloves, roughly chopped

1 sprig rosemary, leaves finely chopped, plus 4 sprigs rosemary

1 whole preserved lemon, rinsed and dried thoroughly, then thinly sliced

4 tablespoons olive oil

1 tablespoon plain (all-purpose) flour

500 ml (17 fl oz/2 cups) chicken stock

1 Preheat the oven to 160°C (320°F). Score the skin of the lamb with a knife, spacing the score marks about 2 cm ($\frac{3}{4}$ inch) apart and cutting about halfway through the fat. Rub lots of salt and pepper all over the lamb.

2 To make the marinade, put the garlic, chopped rosemary, three-quarters of the preserved lemon (save the rest for the gravy) and 2 tablespoons of the olive oil in a bowl and mix well. Using your hands, rub two-thirds of the mixture all over the lamb until well coated. Place a rosemary sprig on top of the lamb, then truss it with kitchen string to form a log.

3 Place the remaining 3 rosemary sprigs in the base of a roasting dish, then spread the remaining marinade in the dish. Sit the lamb, skin side up, on top of the rosemary. Cover with 2 layers of foil, making sure it is tightly sealed so that it becomes a steaming chamber when it cooks. Put the dish in the oven and slow-roast the lamb for 4 hours. Remove the lamb from the oven and transfer to a tray, cover loosely with foil and leave to rest for 10 minutes before carving.

4 Meanwhile, strain the juices in the roasting dish through a fine sieve into a saucepan. Spoon off the excess fat, place the pan over medium heat to warm through, then whisk in the flour and cook for 1 minute. Add the chicken stock and whisk until the flour has dissolved and the gravy has thickened. Add the remaining quarter of preserved lemon to the gravy, stir well and then pour into a serving jug. Cut the lamb into 1.5 cm ($\frac{5}{8}$ inch) thick slices and serve the gravy on the side.

'OH THE WEATHER OUTSIDE IS FRIGHTFUL, BUT THE FIRE IS SO DELIGHTFUL, AND SINCE WE'VE NO PLACE TO GO, COOK IT SLOW, COOK IT SLOW, COOK IT SLOW!' YES, NOTHING BEATS A SLOW-BRAISED LAMB SHANK STEW IN WINTER, WITH BUTTERY PUFF PASTRY TO SOAK UP ALL THE BEAUTIFUL SAUCE. NOW ALL YOU NEED IS A GLASS OF RED AND A GOOD DVD OR SOME MUSIC.

Lamb shank pie

4 lamb shanks

4 tablespoons plain
(all-purpose) flour,
for dusting

4 tablespoons olive oil

40 g (1½ oz) butter

3 carrots, diced

2 celery stalks, diced

2 onions, diced

5 garlic cloves, roughly
chopped

250 ml (8½ fl oz/1 cup) veal
stock

about 375 ml (13 fl oz/
1½ cups) red wine

2 bay leaves

3 sprigs thyme, leaves
picked

salt and freshly ground
black pepper, to taste

2 tablespoons flat-leaf
(Italian) parsley, finely
chopped

4 sheets puff pastry

1 egg, lightly beaten for
egg wash

1 Dust the lamb shanks with the flour, then shake off any excess flour. Heat the olive oil in a large pot over medium–high heat and brown the lamb shanks on all sides. Remove and set aside.

2 Melt the butter in the same pot, then add the carrots, celery, onions and garlic, and sauté for 5 minutes until caramelised. Pour in the veal stock to deglaze the pot, then return the lamb shanks to the pot. Pour in enough red wine until the lamb shanks are fully submerged (you'll need about half a bottle of wine, perhaps a bit more). Add the bay leaves and thyme, turn the heat down to low and braise the lamb shanks for 2 hours, or until the meat falls off the bone.

3 Remove the lamb shanks from the pot and shred the meat off the bones, then return the meat to the pot. Season with salt and pepper, sprinkle with parsley and mix well. Set the bones aside.

4 Preheat the oven to 200°C (400°F). Divide the lamb stew among 4 heatproof bowls, then insert a lamb bone upright in the centre of each bowl.

5 Make a small hole in the centre of each pastry sheet, just big enough for the bone to slide through, then line up the hole over the bone and gently lower the pastry onto the bowl. Fold the corners of the pastry inward towards the bone, then pinch the pastry along the rim of the bowl to seal. Brush the pastry with the egg wash, then bake for 20–25 minutes, or until the pastry is golden brown.

I MAY SOUND LIKE A BROKEN RECORD, BUT CEREAL BUTTER PRAWNS HAS TO BE MY ALL-TIME FAVOURITE PRAWN DISH! THIS WAS POPULAR IN MALAYSIA IN THE 80S, AND EVEN TODAY IT HOLDS A PLACE IN MANY PEOPLE'S HEARTS. THIS RECIPE IS A DEVIATION FROM THE ORIGINAL, WHICH USES A LOT MORE BUTTER IN COOKING TO CREATE STRANDS OF EGG FLOSS USED TO COAT THE PRAWNS. THE ADDICTIVELY CRUNCHY, TOASTY BITS YOU SEE HERE ARE THANKS TO THE WHEAT CEREAL, WHICH IS LIGHTER AND NOT AS CLOYING.

Cereal butter PRAWNS

500 g (1 lb 2 oz) raw large king prawns (shrimp), unpeeled
½ egg, beaten
3 tablespoons plain (all-purpose) flour
vegetable oil, for deep-frying
50 g (2 oz/1 cup) wheat cereal, toasted (see note)
4 tablespoons milk powder (optional)

2 tablespoons icing (confectioners') sugar
1 teaspoon salt
pinch of ground white pepper
70 g (2½ oz) butter, at room temperature
3 sprigs curry leaves
3 bird's eye chillies, thinly sliced

1 Trim the prawn legs with scissors, then cut along the spine and remove the intestinal tract. Rinse the prawns and pat dry thoroughly with paper towel. Place the prawns in a bowl, add the egg and mix well, then sprinkle with the flour, adding a little bit at a time, mixing until all the prawns are well coated.

2 Pour the vegetable oil into a large wok until about half full, then heat the oil to 180°C (350°F) over medium–high heat. Test to see if the oil is hot enough by dipping a wooden chopstick into the hot oil — if the oil starts steadily bubbling around the chopstick, it's ready. Working in batches so you don't overcrowd the wok, deep-fry the prawns for about 2 minutes until crispy and golden. Drain on paper towel and set aside.

3 Put the wheat cereal, milk powder (if using), icing sugar, salt and white pepper in a bowl and mix well.

4 Wipe the wok clean, then add the butter and melt over medium–low heat. Add the curry leaves and chillies and fry for 30 seconds until fragrant. Add the cereal mixture and stir until fragrant, then add the prawns and toss them well to coat in the crispy cereal. Transfer to a serving plate and serve with steamed rice.

Note: The cereal used in this recipe is Nestlé Nestum wholegrain wheat cereal. It is in granule form and is very light and crumbly. Look for it in Asian grocers or, alternatively, use any non-sweetened wheat cereal such as Weetbix; pulse it in the blender until it resembles coarse crumbs.

Nyonya SPICY TAMARIND snapper

1 whole snapper (about 1.2 kg/2 lb 10 oz)
salt, to taste
75 g (2½ oz/½ cup) plain (all-purpose)
  flour
vegetable oil, for deep-frying

125 ml (4 fl oz/½ cup) Rempah spice
  paste (page 272)
2 tablespoons tamarind purée mixed
  with 125 ml (4 fl oz/½ cup) hot water

1 Clean the fish and pat dry thoroughly with paper towel. Make three deep cuts into the flesh of the fish on both sides. Rub salt all over the fish, and inside the cavity as well. Put the flour on a plate and dredge the fish in the flour until well coated, shaking off any excess.

2 Pour the vegetable oil into a large wok until about half full, then heat the oil to 180°C (350°F) over medium–high heat. Test to see if the oil is hot enough by dipping a wooden chopstick into the hot oil — if the oil starts steadily bubbling around the chopstick, it's ready. Gently lower the fish into the hot oil, head first, and

deep-fry for 4–5 minutes on each side, depending on the size of the fish, until golden brown (see tip). Remove and place on a wire rack over a baking tray to drain.

3 Tip the oil out of the wok, leaving only 3 tablespoons in the wok. Add the rempah spice paste and fry for about 5 minutes until fragrant. Pour in the tamarind water and bring to the boil, then reduce the heat and simmer until the liquid has reduced by half. Transfer the fish to a serving plate, then pour the spicy tamarind sauce over the fish. Serve with steamed rice.

Tip: When deep-frying large fish in a wok, first cook the fish on one side, then lift it out using a large deep-frying ladle. Carefully flip the fish over using kitchen tongs, then lower the ladle into the hot oil and carefully slip the fish back into the wok.

SNAPPER — THE FISH WITH A GIANT FOREHEAD — IS ONE OF THE BEST FISH TO EAT IN AUSTRALIA AND IS AVAILABLE ALL YEAR ROUND. I LOVE COOKING THE SNAPPER WHOLE, BECAUSE THERE'S JUST SOMETHING BEAUTIFUL ABOUT EATING A WHOLE FISH FROM HEAD TO TAIL. EVERYONE SEEMS TO HAVE THEIR FAVOURITE PART OF THE FISH; I LOVE GNAWING ON THE DEEP-FRIED CRISPY TAIL WHILE MY FRIEND HELEN WILL GO FOR THE EYEBALLS! SO IT'S A WIN-WIN SITUATION FOR EVERYONE.

SERVES
4

SOFT SHELL CRABS ARE CRABS THAT HAVE MOULTED FROM THEIR OLD SHELLS AND ARE STILL SOFT. THERE IS VERY LITTLE CLEANING NEEDED, EXCEPT TO REMOVE THE FEATHERY GILLS, ALSO KNOWN AS DEAD MAN'S FINGERS. THERE IS SIMPLY NO BETTER WAY TO COOK SOFT SHELL CRAB THAN DEEP-FRYING IT AND EATING IT WHOLE! A SPICY AND TANGY SALAD LIKE SOM TUM (GREEN PAPAYA SALAD) IS THE PERFECT ACCOMPANIMENT FOR CRAB OR ANY DEEP-FRIED FOOD, AS ITS TARTNESS CUTS THROUGH THE FAT LIKE A SAMURAI SWORD.

DEEP-FRIED *soft shell crab* *with* SOM TUM

4 soft shell crabs
155 g (5½ oz/1 cup)
    potato starch
1 teaspoon salt
1 teaspoon ground
    white pepper
1 egg, beaten
vegetable oil, for
    deep-frying

SOM TUM
1 garlic clove, peeled
2 bird's eye chillies
1 teaspoon dried
    shrimp, soaked in hot
    water for 10 minutes
    then drained
2 tablespoons lime juice
2 tablespoons fish sauce
1 tablespoon grated
    palm sugar (jaggery)

2 snake (long) beans,
    cut into 5 cm (2 inch)
    lengths
450 g (1 lb) green
    papaya, peeled and
    shredded
10 cherry tomatoes,
    halved
35 g (1¼ oz/¼ cup)
    peanuts, toasted and
    roughly chopped

1 To make the som tum, pound the garlic and chillies in a mortar and pestle until crushed, then add the dried shrimp and pound until softened. Add the lime juice, fish sauce and palm sugar, and stir until the sugar has dissolved. Add the beans, green papaya and tomatoes, and pound gently just to bruise and soften the vegetables. Have a taste and adjust the flavour of the salad according to your liking — there should be a balance of sweet, sour, spicy and a little bit of salty. Finally, add the toasted peanuts and mix well.

2 To clean the soft shell crabs, pull the little flap on the underside off and remove all the guts inside. Using a pair of kitchen scissors, trim the head off to remove the eyes and the mouth, which can taste bitter. Flip one side of the shell over without removing it, then pull off the feathery gills underneath, then repeat the same on the other side. Rinse and pat dry with paper towel.

3 Cut each crab in half. Combine the potato starch, salt and white pepper in a bowl, and the beaten egg in another. Dip each crab piece in egg, then dredge in the potato starch until well coated, shaking off any excess.

4 Pour the oil into a large saucepan until about half full, then heat the oil to 180°C (350°F) over medium–high heat. Test to see if the oil is hot enough by dipping a wooden chopstick into the hot oil — if the oil starts steadily bubbling around the chopstick, it's ready. Deep-fry the crab in batches until crispy and golden brown, then drain on paper towel. Divide the salad among 4 plates and top each with 2 pieces of soft shell crab

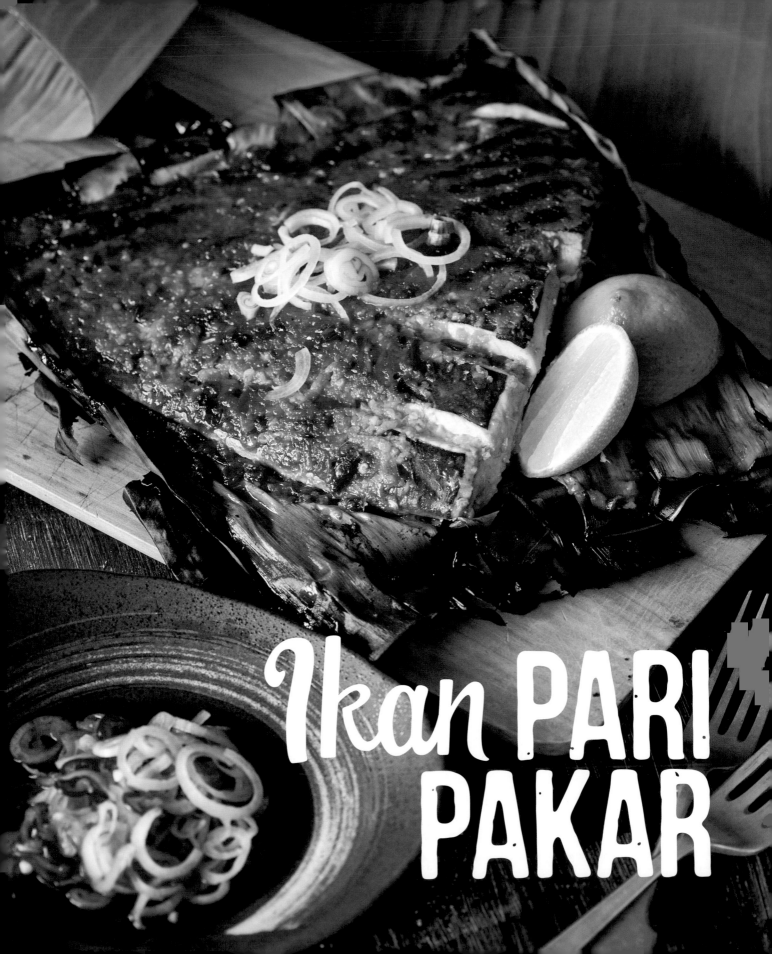

Ikan PARI PAKAR

I LOVE SUPPER TIME IN MALAYSIA AND I'M NOT TALKING ABOUT DINNER. SUPPER IN SOUTHEAST ASIAN COUNTRIES REFERS TO THE MEAL AFTER DINNER, USUALLY AFTER 9PM. AS THE TEMPERATURE STARTS TO COOL, PLASTIC TABLES AND CHAIRS SLOWLY SPREAD OUT ONTO THE STREETS, AND ALLURING SCENTS OF DELICIOUS FOOD DRIFT THROUGH THE AIR FROM THE ROWS OF HAWKER STANDS. I LOVE THE HAWKER FOOD SCENE, AND GRILLED SKATE WING IS WHAT I USUALLY ORDER.

300–400 g (10½–14 oz) piece
    of skate wing
juice of 1 lemon
pinch of salt
1 large piece banana leaf
a few toothpicks
1 French shallot, thinly
    sliced
wedge of lime

SPICY DRESSING
125 ml (4 fl oz/½ cup)
    vegetable oil
250 ml (8½ fl oz/1 cup)
    Rempah spice paste
    (page 272)
2 tablespoons tamarind purée
2 tablespoons sugar
pinch of salt
125 ml (4 fl oz/½ cup) water

CHILLI SHALLOT DRESSING
1 large red chilli, finely
    chopped
2 French shallots, thinly
    sliced
2 tablespoons light soy
    sauce
juice of ½ lime

SERVES
2

1 Clean the skate, pat dry with paper towel, then place it on a large plate. Make a few long, deep cuts into the flesh of the fish on both sides. Rub the fish with the lemon juice and salt, cover with plastic wrap, and put in the refrigerator to marinate for 10 minutes.

2 Meanwhile, to make the spicy dressing, heat the vegetable oil in a frying pan over medium–high heat. Add the rempah spice paste and stir-fry for about 5 minutes until fragrant, then add the tamarind purée, sugar, salt and water. Reduce the heat to medium and simmer until the sauce thickens. Remove from the heat and leave the sauce in the pan to cool completely.

3 Run hot water over the banana leaf to soften it, then pat dry with paper towel.

Place the banana leaf on the work surface, matte side up. Spread half the spicy dressing on the leaf, lay the skate on top, then spoon the remaining dressing on the fish. Fold the banana leaf into a parcel to enclose the fish, and secure it with toothpicks.

4 Heat up a barbecue grill or chargrill pan and cook the fish parcel for about 12–15 minutes, turning it over once halfway through cooking time. Meanwhile, make the chilli shallot dressing by simply mixing all the ingredients together.

5 When the fish is ready, place the banana leaf parcel on a serving plate and open up the parcel. Garnish with the shallot and squeeze the lime wedge over the fish. Serve the dressing on the side.

{GRILLED SPICY SKATE WING IN BANANA LEAF}

Burnt butter LOBSTER TAIL with apple & salmon roe

SERVES
2

READ MY LIPS: KEEP IT SIMPLE, KEEP IT SIMPLE, KEEP IT SIMPLE! THE BEST WAY TO COOK A LOBSTER IS TO KEEP IT SIMPLE. YOU DON'T WANT A RECIPE WITH INTENSE FLAVOURS THAT OVERPOWER THE SWEETNESS OF THE LOBSTER MEAT; IT SHOULD BE ENJOYED FOR ITS NATURAL FLAVOURS. AND THEY DON'T COME CHEAP, SO TREAT THE LOBSTER WITH RESPECT AND DON'T OVERCOOK IT; OTHERWISE, YOU'LL JUST HAVE WASHED YOUR MONEY DOWN THE DRAIN AND TOTALLY WASTED A GOOD LOBSTER.

1 Granny Smith apple, julienned into matchsticks

juice of 1 lemon

salt, to taste

125 ml (4 fl oz/½ cup) olive oil

1 bunch basil leaves

50 g (2 oz) butter

1 cooked lobster tail, shell removed then halved

4 tablespoons Wasabi mayo (page 270), poured into a squeeze bottle or piping bag

1 heaped tablespoon salmon roe

baby flat-leaf (Italian) parsley, as garnish

1 Put the grated apple into a bowl, squeeze the lemon all over, season with salt to taste, then stir well. Cover with plastic wrap and place in the refrigerator.

2 Heat the olive oil in a small saucepan over medium–low heat, add the basil leaves and cook for 2 minutes. Turn the heat off and let the leaves infuse in the oil for 20 minutes, then strain through a fine sieve and discard the solids. Set side for later use.

3 Melt the butter in a frying pan over medium heat. When the butter starts to froth and turn a nutty brown, immediately turn the heat down to low, and place the lobster tail halves in the pan and cook for 2 minutes, turning once. While the lobster is cooking, use a tablespoon to douse the burnt butter over the lobster regularly. Turn the heat off and transfer the lobster to a tray, reserving the burnt butter sauce.

4 To serve, place a handful of apple salad on a plate. Cut the lobster into 2 cm (¾ inch) thick slices and place on top of the salad. Drizzle burnt butter sauce over the lobster. Add dollops of wasabi mayonnaise around the lobster, garnish with salmon roe and baby parsley, then drizzle with the basil-infused oil.

SERVES
2

Golden sand mud crab

NORMALLY I WILL ONLY COOK WITH LIVE MUD CRABS WHEN THEY ARE IN SEASON DURING SUMMER. I AM LUCKY TO LIVE ON THE NEW SOUTH WALES COAST AND THE MUD CRABS CAUGHT LOCALLY ARE SOME OF THE BEST I'VE EVER TASTED.

GOLDEN SAND MUD CRAB, WIDELY KNOWN AS MUD CRAB TOSSED IN SALTED DUCK EGG, IS ANOTHER POPULAR SINGAPOREAN AND MALAYSIAN DISH. THE CRAB IS LIGHTLY BATTERED AND DEEP-FRIED, THEN COATED IN A CARPET OF GOLDEN SALTED EGG YOLK. DON'T BE AFRAID TO GET YOUR HANDS DIRTY; LICK EVERY SURFACE OF THE SHELL THEN PRISE OPEN THE CLAWS AND SUCK ALL THE SWEET MEAT OUT. THERE'S SIMPLY NO BETTER WAY TO DEVOUR A CRAB.

1 large fresh or live mud crab (about 1 kg/2 lb 3 oz) (see notes)

1 egg, beaten

120 g (4¼ oz/1 cup) tapioca starch (or use potato starch or plain flour)

vegetable oil, for deep-frying

30 g (1 oz) butter, at room temperature

5 sprigs curry leaves

3 bird's eye chillies, thinly sliced

1 tablespoon sugar

50 g (2 oz) salted duck egg yolks, mashed (see notes)

Notes: If using live crabs, make sure you prepare them humanely by putting them to sleep in the freezer for 1 hour beforehand.

Salted duck eggs are available in Asian grocers; they usually come already hard-boiled and cured. You only need the egg yolks for this dish, but you can use the egg whites for another dish — serve them with congee (page 204), for instance. If the yolks are too firm, put them in the microwave and heat for a minute, then mash them with a fork.

1 To prepare the crabs, scrub them well to remove any dirt and algae. Lift the abdomen (the triangle flap) on the underside and you will be able to pull the top shell off. Remove all the feather-like gills and the mouthparts, and clean the shell thoroughly.

2 Using a cleaver, chop the crab in half down the centre, then cut each piece in half again. There will be some black stuff inside the crab, which you need to remove as well. Trim off the hairy pointy tip of the legs, then crack the 2 large claws with the back of the cleaver. Pat dry thoroughly with some paper towel.

3 Put the crab pieces and beaten egg in a large mixing bowl. Stir to mix well, then dip each crab piece into the tapioca starch, patting the crab gently until well coated in the starch.

4 Pour the vegetable oil into a large wok until about half full, then heat the oil to 180°C (350°F) over medium–high heat. Test to see if the oil is hot enough by dipping a wooden chopstick into the hot oil — if the oil starts steadily bubbling around the chopstick, it's ready. Working in batches so you don't overcrowd the wok, deep-fry the crab pieces for about 5 minutes, or until the shells turn red and form a nice golden crispy crust on the outside. Remove from the wok and drain on a rack over a tray.

5 Drain the oil from the wok and wipe clean. Reheat the wok, then add the butter, curry leaves and chillies, and stir-fry over medium heat until fragrant. Add the sugar and mashed egg yolks and keep stirring: the butter will start to froth up and will become lighter in colour. Return the crab to the wok and toss everything together a few times until all the pieces of crab are nicely coated in the sauce. Pile the crab onto a large serving plate and serve immediately.

CHAPTER 5

Rice & NOODLES

Nasi lemak ❖ BAN MEE {HAND-PULLED FLAT NOODLES} ❖ Billy's special fried rice ❖ CLAYPOT CHICKEN & MUSHROOM RICE ❖ Pork & chive wonton noodle ❖ Pork & chive dumpling noodle soup ❖ ZHA JIANG NOODLES ❖ Char kuey kak ❖ Char kuey teow ❖ PORK MINCE BALLS & CENTURY EGGS CONGEE ❖ Penang har mee (Prawn noodle soup) ❖ Curry laksa ❖ Assam laksa (spicy & sour fish stock laksa)

RICE AND NOODLES ARE THE HEART AND SOUL OF CHINESE CUISINE; THEY ARE THE STAPLE ACCOMPANIMENT, THE CARRIER OF SAUCES AND THE PALATE CLEANSER BETWEEN FLAVOURS.

NASI lemak

MY PALATE WAS TRAINED TO TAKE SPICY HOT FOOD AT A VERY YOUNG AGE BY EATING LOTS OF NASI LEMAK, THE NATIONAL DISH OF MALAYSIA. NASI LEMAK DIRECTLY TRANSLATES AS 'FATTY RICE', A NAME DERIVED FROM THE PROCESS OF COOKING THE RICE IN RICH COCONUT CREAM.

SERVES
4-6

COCONUT RICE

300 g (10½ oz/1½ cups)
  jasmine rice
2 slices of ginger
2 pandan (screw pine)
  leaves, knotted (see note
  page 93)
125 ml (4 fl oz/½ cup) coconut
  cream
pinch of salt

SAMBAL BELACHAN PASTE

20 g (¾ oz) belachan (dried
  shrimp paste)
150 g (5 oz) large fresh
  red chillies
juice of 3 limes
salt, to taste

SAMBAL IKAN BILIS

3 tablespoons vegetable oil
50 g (2 oz) ikan bilis (dried
  anchovies)
1 brown onion, thinly sliced
125 g (4 oz/½ cup) sambal
  belachan paste
pinch of salt
1 tablespoon sugar

FRIED PEANUTS AND ANCHOVIES

125 ml (4 fl oz/½ cup)
  vegetable oil
50 g (2 oz/⅓ cup) raw
  peanuts, skins on
30 g (1 oz) ikan bilis (dried
  anchovies)
1 tablespoon caster
  (superfine) sugar

vegetable oil, for deep-frying
4 hard-boiled eggs, peeled
4 banana leaves, used as
  serving mat (optional)
1 Lebanese (short)
  cucumber, thinly sliced

1 To make the coconut rice, wash and rinse the rice several times until the water runs clear. Put the rice, ginger, pandan leaves, coconut cream and salt in a large saucepan, then top with enough water to come up 2 cm (¾ inch) above the level of the rice. Boil the rice over medium heat until most of the liquid has absorbed and bubbles start to appear on the surface. Cover, turn the heat down to low and steam for 10 minutes. Remove from the heat and let it steam for a further 10 minutes (do not open the lid). Fluff the rice with a rice paddle or fork, then put the lid back on to keep the rice warm until ready to serve.

2 To make the sambal belachan paste, wrap the belachan in foil and toast in a frying pan for 2 minutes on each side. Cool before removing the foil. Pound the belachan, chillies and lime juice together in a mortar and pestle or blend in a food processor to form a fine paste. Season with salt, to taste.

3 To make the sambal ikan bilis, heat the vegetable oil in a frying pan over medium–high heat and fry the anchovies for about 2 minutes until crispy and golden brown. Add the onion and fry until soft and translucent, then add the sambal belachan paste and cook for 3 minutes, stirring until everything is well coated. Season with the salt and sugar, cook for a further minute, then transfer to a serving plate.

4 To make the fried peanuts and anchovies, heat the vegetable oil in a frying pan over medium heat and fry the peanuts for about 1 minute until golden brown. Strain the oil into a bowl to be reused, and spread the peanuts on a tray lined with paper towel. Pour the oil back into the frying pan and reheat it. Now fry the dried anchovies for 2 minutes until crispy and golden. Drain the oil and spread the fried anchovies on the tray with the peanuts. Put the peanuts and anchovies into a bowl and sprinkle with the sugar, tossing to mix well.

5 Pour the vegetable oil into a medium saucepan until about half full, then heat the oil to 180°C (350°F) over medium–high heat. Test to see if the oil is hot enough by dipping a wooden chopstick into the hot oil — if the oil starts steadily bubbling around the chopstick, it's ready. Gently drop the eggs into the hot oil and fry them for about 2 minutes, or until golden brown, then remove and drain on paper towel.

6 Wipe the banana leaves with a damp cloth, then brush with vegetable oil. Fill a small bowl with the coconut rice and tip it onto the leaf, then serve with sambal ikan bilis, fried peanuts and anchovies, a few slices of cucumber, and a deep-fried egg with a dollop of sambal belachan paste on top.

Ban mee
{HAND-PULLED FLAT NOODLES}

MY ANCESTORS ARE FROM FUJIAN PROVINCE IN CHINA, AND THIS HUMBLE HOKKIEN NOODLE DISH IS VERY CLOSE TO MY HEART. I CALL IT THE 'PASTA OF THE EAST' AS THE INGREDIENTS TO MAKE THE EGG NOODLES ARE SIMILAR TO THOSE OF PASTA. YOU CAN DEFINITELY USE A PASTA MACHINE TO CUT THE NOODLES EVENLY, BUT I PREFER TO USE MY FINGERS AND PULL THE NOODLE INTO BITE-SIZED PIECES, IN KEEPING WITH ITS RUSTIC ORIGINS.

SERVES

4

200 g (7 oz) pork loin medallion, thinly sliced
2 tablespoons light soy sauce, plus extra to serve
1 teaspoon sesame oil
1 tablespoon cornflour (cornstarch)
3 tablespoons vegetable oil
30 g (1 oz) ikan bilis (dried anchovies)
1 bunch of sweet potato leaves, washed (see note)
handful of garlic chives, cut into 5 cm (2 inch) lengths
4–5 dried shiitake mushrooms, soaked in hot water for 1 hour, stalks discarded, thinly sliced
3 bird's eye chillies, finely chopped

NOODLES

300 g (10½ oz/2 cups) plain (all-purpose) flour, plus extra for dusting
pinch of salt
1 egg
3 tablespoons water
1 teaspoon sesame oil

ANCHOVY SOUP BASE

2 litres (68 fl oz/8 cups) water
30 g (1 oz) ikan bilis (dried anchovies)
185 g (6½ oz/1 cup) dried soya beans
1 tablespoon sesame oil
3 tablespoons soy sauce, or to taste

1 To make the noodles, combine the flour and salt in a large mixing bowl, then make a well in the centre. Crack the egg into the well, then add the water and sesame oil. Using a fork, slowly stir the mixture until everything comes together to form a dough. Transfer the dough to a lightly floured work surface and knead the dough until it is smooth. Place the dough back in the bowl, cover with plastic wrap and refrigerate for at least 1 hour.

2 Meanwhile, to make the anchovy soup base, pour the water into a large pot, then add the dried anchovies and soya beans and bring to the boil over medium–high heat. Then reduce the heat to low and simmer for 1 hour. Season with sesame oil and soy sauce to taste, and strain the stock into another clean pot, discarding the solids. Keep the soup warm over very low heat while preparing the rest of the ingredients.

3 Combine the pork, soy sauce, sesame oil and cornflour in a bowl. Cover and place in the refrigerator to marinate for 20 minutes.

4 Heat the vegetable oil in a frying pan over medium–high heat and fry the dried anchovies until golden brown and crispy. Drain on paper towel and set aside to cool.

5 Bring the soup base back to a rolling boil over high heat. Divide the dough into 4 portions, then lightly dust each with flour so it doesn't stick to your hands. Using your fingers, slowly pinch one end of the dough until it is about 2 mm (⅛ inch) thick, then pull off a bite-sized piece and drop it into the soup. Repeat the process until all the dough is used, pinching off one dough piece at a time and dropping it into the soup. Cook the noodles for about 1 minute, or until they float to the surface. Ladle them out with a small wire sieve and transfer to a serving bowl. Repeat with the remaining 3 portions of dough.

6 Place a few pork strips in a small wire sieve and drop them into the hot soup. Cook for 1 minute, then add a small handful each of sweet potato leaves and garlic chives and scald them for 30 seconds. Drain and transfer the cooked ingredients to the bowl. Repeat with the remaining pork, sweet potato leaves and garlic chives to make another 3 portions. Ladle some hot soup over the noodles, then garnish with some mushrooms and the fried anchovies.

7 Combine the chopped chillies and extra soy sauce in a small dipping bowl and serve on the side with the noodles.

Note: Traditionally ban mee is served with sweet potato leaves, which are available from Asian grocers. They can be substituted with any leafy green, such as choy sum, water spinach, English spinach or en choy.

BILLY'S SPECIAL *fried rice*

3 tablespoons vegetable
   oil
2 garlic cloves, finely
   chopped
2 lap cheong (Chinese
   sausages, see note
   page 94), thinly sliced
6 scallops, roe removed,
   cut into small cubes
2 eggs, mixed with

3 tablespoons water,
   lightly beaten
750 g (1 lb 10 oz/4 cups)
   cold cooked jasmine
   rice (see notes)
150 g (5 oz/1½ cups)
   frozen peas
1 large carrot, peeled
   and cut into small
   cubes

3 tablespoons light soy
   sauce
1 tablespoon dark soy
   caramel
1 teaspoon sesame oil
1 teaspoon ground
   white pepper
20 g (¾ oz) tobiko roe
   (see notes)

1 Heat half of the vegetable oil in a
wok over high heat. Add the garlic
and stir-fry until fragrant. Add the lap
cheong and scallops and stir-fry for 1
minute until the sausages are slightly
crisp and the scallops are just cooked
through. Remove and set aside.

2 Heat the remaining oil in the wok
over high heat. Pour in the egg
mixture and leave to fry on one side.
While the egg is still a little runny on
top, add the rice, peas and carrot to
cover the egg, then turn the heat down
to medium. Give everything a gentle
stir with a spatula, so that some of the
fried egg coats the rice. Add the soy
sauce, dark soy caramel, sesame oil
and white pepper, and stir-fry until
the rice is well coated. Return the

lap cheong and scallops to the wok,
toss to combine, then remove the wok
from the heat.

3 Place the tobiko roe in the bottom
of a large serving bowl, then fill
the bowl to the brim with the fried
rice. Place an upside-down serving
plate over the bowl, then carefully
pick up both the plate and bowl and
flip it over. Remove the bowl.

*Notes: Fried rice is best made with cold rice that
has been stored in the refrigerator overnight.
Avoid using freshly cooked rice, as this contains a
lot of moisture and will result in gluggy fried rice.*

*Tobiko roe, also known as flying fish roe, is
commonly used in sushi. It can be found in most
Asian grocers.*

FRIED RICE IS A NO-BRAINER AND I TRUST EVERYONE KNOWS HOW TO COOK A GOOD FRIED RICE. BUT INSTEAD OF USING THE USUAL FROZEN PEAS, PRAWNS AND THIN STRIPS OF HAM, TRY TO CREATE YOUR OWN VERSION AND USE INGREDIENTS THAT ARE A LITTLE DIFFERENT: SALTED FISH, LAP CHEONG, SALTED RADISH, FISH CAKE SLICES OR EVEN CENTURY EGG — THE POSSIBILITIES ARE ENDLESS! THIS IS MY VERSION THAT I LIKE TO COOK — SOMETHING A LITTLE BIT FANCY FOR A SPECIAL OCCASION SUCH AS LUNAR NEW YEAR.

SERVES
4

Claypot chicken & MUSHROOM RICE

CLAYPOT COOKING IS AN ANCIENT COOKING TECHNIQUE THAT HAS BEEN AROUND SINCE ROMAN TIMES. THE CLAYPOT NEEDS TO BE SOAKED IN WATER BEFORE EACH USE, SO IT RELEASES STEAM DURING THE COOKING PROCESS, CREATING A TENDER, FLAVOURFUL DISH. WHEN THE CHICKEN RICE IS COOKED IN THE CLAYPOT, THE BOTTOM LAYER WILL YIELD A CARAMELISED CRUST FROM THE SOY SAUCES. ALTERNATIVELY, YOU CAN ALSO USE A SMALL DUTCH OVEN OR CAST-IRON POT.

5 dried shiitake mushrooms
2 boneless, skinless chicken thighs, cut into cubes
1 teaspoon sesame oil
1 tablespoon light soy sauce, plus extra to serve
1 tablespoon oyster sauce
1 teaspoon cornflour (cornstarch)
200 g (7 oz/1 cup) jasmine rice
2 tablespoons vegetable oil
1 garlic clove, finely chopped
5 pieces thinly sliced ginger

1 tablespoon dried shrimp, soaked in hot water for 10 minutes, then drained and dried (optional)
3 anchovies, roughly chopped (optional)
2 lap cheong (Chinese sausages, see note page 94), thinly sliced on the diagonal
1 spring onion (scallion), thinly sliced
fried shallots, for garnish

COOKING STOCK
250 ml (8½ fl oz/1 cup) water (from soaking the mushrooms)
1 tablespoon dark soy caramel
1 tablespoon oyster sauce
2 tablespoons light soy sauce
1 teaspoon sesame oil

1 Soak the shiitake mushrooms in a bowl of hot water for 1 hour until softened, then drain, reserving 250 ml (8½ fl oz/1 cup) of the mushroom water for later use. Remove the mushroom stalks.

2 Put the chicken cubes in a mixing bowl. Combine the sesame oil, soy sauce, oyster sauce and cornflour, then pour over the chicken and stir to coat in the marinade. Set aside to marinate for 10 minutes while preparing the rest of the ingredients.

3 Wash the rice in cold water a few times until the water runs clear, then drain.

4 Heat the vegetable oil in a claypot over low heat and gradually bring it up to medium–high heat. Add the garlic and ginger, and the dried shrimp and anchovies if using, and fry until fragrant. Then add the lap cheong and chicken and cook for a further 3–5 minutes until lightly coloured. Add the rice and mushrooms and stir well.

5 To make the cooking stock, mix the reserved mushroom water with the remaining ingredients.

6 Pour about 3 tablespoons of the cooking stock into the claypot to deglaze it; stir to make sure nothing is sticking to the bottom of the claypot, then pour in the remaining stock, stir well and bring to the boil. Once boiling, immediately put the lid on, then turn the heat down to low and cook for 15 minutes. Turn the heat off and let it rest for 10 minutes. It is crucial not to open the lid at this point, as the rice is still being cooked and steamed with the residue heat inside the claypot.

7 Fluff up the rice with a fork, garnish with spring onion and fried shallots, and give it another good splash of light soy sauce before serving.

SERVES
2

Pork and chive
dumpling noodle soup

Pork and chive
wonton noodles

Pork & chive WONTON NOODLES

(DRY VERSION)

2 litres (68 fl oz/8 cups) water

salt, to taste

1 chicken stock cube

2 spring onions (scallions), thinly sliced

425 g (15 oz) packet fresh egg noodles

1 bunch choy sum, ends trimmed, washed and cut into 5 cm (2 inch) lengths

125 ml (4 fl oz/½ cup) light soy sauce, plus extra to serve

4 tablespoons dark soy caramel

ground white pepper

fried shallots, to garnish

Pickled green chillies, as condiment (page 274)

PORK AND CHIVE WONTONS

300 g (10½ oz) minced (ground) pork

1 bunch garlic chives, finely chopped

3 garlic cloves, finely chopped

2 tablespoons light soy sauce

1 teaspoon sesame oil

1 tablespoon cornflour (cornstarch)

1 teaspoon ground white pepper

1 packet square wonton wrappers

THIS BRINGS BACK MEMORIES OF WHEN MY MUM WOULD TAKE MY BROTHER AND ME TO THE LOCAL KOPITIAM (COFFEE HOUSE) FOR BREAKFAST. MY BROTHER USUALLY ASKED FOR CHAR KUEY TEOW (PAGE 200) AND I WOULD ALWAYS GO FOR THE SIMPLE WONTON NOODLE SOUP. EVEN THOUGH THE WONTONS ARE MEANT TO BE EATEN TOGETHER WITH THE NOODLES, I WOULD EAT THE NOODLES FIRST AND THEN THE WONTONS, ALWAYS SAVING THE BEST FOR LAST.

1 To make the wontons, place all the ingredients, except the wrappers, in a bowl and stir to combine. Scoop a teaspoon of the pork mixture and place it in the centre of a wrapper, then bring the wrapper up around the mixture, scrunching it at the top to seal. Repeat with the rest of the pork filling.

2 Pour the water into a large pot and bring to the boil over high heat. Season with salt and the chicken stock cube, stir well and then turn the heat to down to a simmer.

3 Drop the wontons into the hot stock and cook for 3 minutes, then scoop them out and divide among 4 serving bowls. Pour a ladleful of hot stock over the wontons, then garnish with half of the spring onion.

4 Working in 4 batches, place a handful each of egg noodles and choy sum in a wire mesh sieve and dunk it in the hot stock. Cook for 1 minute, then drain and shake off any excess water, and transfer to a serving plate. For each serve, drizzle 1½ tablespoons of soy sauce and 1 tablespoon of dark soy caramel over the top, then sprinkle with some white pepper, spring onion and fried shallots. Serve with a dipping sauce of pickled green chillies in light soy sauce on the side. Serve with the bowls of wonton soup.

Note: Alternatively, instead of cooking the wontons in the hot soup, you can serve them deep-fried.

SERVES

2

- 1 litre (34 fl oz/4 cups) chicken stock
- 1 litre (34 fl oz/4 cups) water
- 5 cm (2 inch) piece ginger, peeled and thinly sliced
- 2 French shallots, thinly sliced
- pinch of ground white pepper
- salt, to taste
- 425 g (15 oz) packet fresh egg noodles
- 1 bunch choy sum, ends trimmed, washed and cut into 5 cm (2 inch) lengths
- 1 spring onion (scallion), thinly sliced
- fried shallots, to garnish

PORK AND CHIVE DUMPLINGS
- 300 g (10½ oz) minced (ground) pork
- 1 bunch garlic chives, finely chopped
- 3 garlic cloves, finely chopped
- 2 tablespoons light soy sauce
- 1 teaspoon sesame oil
- 1 tablespoon cornflour (cornstarch)
- 1 teaspoon ground white pepper
- 1 packet round gowgee wrappers

1 To make the pork and chive dumplings, place all the ingredients, except the wrappers, in a bowl and stir to combine. Scoop a teaspoon of the pork mixture and place it in the centre of a wrapper. Dip your finger in a bowl of water and rub it along the rim of the wrapper, then fold it in half. Crimp the wrapper along the edge, then pinch together to seal. Place the dumpling on a lightly floured tray. Repeat with the rest of the pork filling.

2 Put the chicken stock, water, ginger and shallots in a large saucepan and bring to the boil over high heat. Season the soup with white pepper and salt to taste, then turn the heat to down to a simmer.

3 For each serve, place a handful each of egg noodles and choy sum in a wire mesh sieve and dunk it in the hot soup. Cook for 1 minute, then drain and shake off any excess water, and transfer to a serving bowl. Repeat to make another 3 serves. Drop the dumplings in the hot soup and cook for 3 minutes, then scoop them out and divide among the serving bowls. Ladle hot soup over the noodles and dumplings, then garnish with spring onion and fried shallots.

Note: Alternatively, instead of cooking the dumplings in the hot soup, you can serve them pan-fried. Heat 2 tablespoons oil in a hot frying pan over medium–high heat. Place the dumplings in the pan, then add 3 tablespoons water to the pan and quickly put the lid on and let them steam for 5 minutes. The dumplings will be cooked from the steaming and will be crispy on the bottom from the pan-frying.

SERVES

4

MAKING DUMPLINGS CAN BE VERY THERAPEUTIC, ESPECIALLY WITH A GROUP OF FRIENDS, FOLDING AND CRIMPING THE DUMPLINGS WHILE CHITCHATTING. AND THE TEAM EFFORT WILL BE AMPLY REWARDED WITH A BIG MOUND OF PORK DUMPLINGS.

Pork & chive DUMPLING NOODLE SOUP

Zha jiang NOODLES

THIS SIMPLE NOODLE DISH WAS A STAPLE DURING MY UNI DAYS IN TOOWOOMBA, QUEENSLAND. I LEARNED HOW TO COOK THIS FROM A ROOMMATE OF MINE WHO WAS ORIGINALLY FROM BEIJING. DURING EXAM TIME, WE ALWAYS COOKED A BIG BATCH OF THE ZHA JIANG SAUCE SO IT WOULD LAST US THE WHOLE WEEK. SO, I WOULD LIKE TO DEDICATE THIS NOODLE DISH TO ALL THE UNI STUDENTS OUT THERE — GIVE 2-MINUTE INSTANT NOODLES THE FLICK AND WHIP THESE NOODLES UP IN NO TIME INSTEAD!

3 tablespoons vegetable oil

3 garlic cloves, finely chopped

5 dried red chillies, seeded and finely chopped

1 large fresh red chilli, seeded and finely chopped

500 g (1 lb 2 oz) minced (ground) pork

1 bunch enoki mushrooms (100 g/3½ oz), trimmed

50 g (2 oz/½ cup) brown bean paste (see notes)

250 ml (8½ fl oz/1 cup) water

1 tablespoon dark soy caramel

2 tablespoons sugar

2 tablespoons Shaoxing rice wine

500 g (1 lb 2 oz) packet fresh Shanghai noodles (see notes)

1 carrot, shredded

1 large green cucumber, shredded and drained on paper towel

1 spring onion (scallion), thinly sliced

1 Heat the vegetable oil in a wok over medium–high heat and fry the garlic and chillies for 1 minute, or until fragrant. Add the pork mince and cook for 5 minutes, stirring occasionally and breaking up any lumps, until the mince is brown. Add the enoki mushrooms and cook for a further minute.

2 Add the bean paste and stir until all the mince is nicely coated, then add the water, dark soy caramel, sugar and rice wine, stirring well. Reduce the heat to medium and simmer for 10 minutes, or until the sauce thickens.

3 Meanwhile, bring half a pot of water to the boil, then add the noodles and cook for 3–4 minutes. Drain in a colander and shake off the excess water.

4 Divide the noodles among serving bowls. Pour a ladleful of the mince sauce over the noodles, and serve with a handful each of shredded carrot and cucumber on the side. Garnish with spring onion.

Notes: Brown bean paste, or dou ban jiang in Chinese, is fermented soy bean paste. It can be very salty, so use it sparingly. The bean paste is also available in a chilli version — for those who like it hot!

Shanghai noodles are thick round rice noodles popular in northern China. Shanghai noodles are available from major supermarket or Asian grocers. Alternatively, they can be substituted with Japanese udon noodles.

CHAR
kuey kak

SERVES
2*

* OR 1 GENEROUSLY

CHAR KUEY KAK IS ALSO KNOWN AS CHAI TAU KWAY AND MEANS 'STIR-FRIED RICE CAKE CUBES'. IT IS ANOTHER VARIATION OF A HAWKER-STYLE NOODLE DISH, AND IS VERY SIMILAR TO ITS MORE FAMOUS COUSIN, CHAR KUEY TEOW (PAGE 202). THE RICE CAKE IS VERY EASY TO MAKE AND ONLY REQUIRES A FEW INGREDIENTS. TRADITIONALLY SHREDDED WHITE RADISH (DAIKON) IS ALSO ADDED, BUT I HAVEN'T USED IT HERE. MANY MALAYSIANS PREFER THIS VERSION OVER THE CHAR KUEY TEOW, AS THE CUBES OF RICE CAKE OFFER A SOFT CHEWY TEXTURE TYPICAL OF CLASSIC CHINESE COMFORT FOOD.

3 tablespoons vegetable oil
2 tablespoons finely chopped garlic
2 or 3 strips salted radish, rinsed and patted dry, finely chopped
1 lap cheong (Chinese sausage, see note page 94), thinly sliced
6 raw prawns (shrimp), peeled and deveined
2 tablespoons light soy sauce
2 teaspoons dark soy caramel
pinch of white pepper
1 egg
handful of bean sprouts
handful of garlic chives, cut into 5 cm (2 inch) lengths
Sriracha chilli sauce, to serve

RICE CAKE
110 g (3¾ oz/⅔ cup) rice flour
2 tablespoons potato starch
220 ml (7½ fl oz) water
1 tablespoon sugar
1 teaspoon salt
1 teaspoon sesame oil
pinch of ground white pepper

1 To make the rice cake, mix the rice flour, potato starch and water together to form a smooth batter. Add the sugar, salt, sesame oil and white pepper, and stir to mix well. Pour the batter into a large pot or wok over medium heat, and stir until the mixture thickens to a wet paste. Remove from the heat, then pour the mixture into an 18 cm (7 inch) square baking tin. Use a greased palette knife to spread the mixture evenly.

2 Place the tin in a steamer or in a wok on a rack over a saucepan of simmering water. Steam the rice cake for 30 minutes; test its readiness by inserting a chopstick into the cake — it should come out clean. Remove the rice from the steamer and set aside to cool to room temperature, then cover and refrigerate to set. Tip the rice cake out onto a board and cut into 1 × 3 cm (½ × 1¼ inch) blocks.

3 Heat 2 tablespoons of the vegetable oil in a non-stick wok over high heat, then add the garlic and strips of salted radish and fry until fragrant. Add the rice cakes and fry, stirring occasionally, until charred with crispy edges on all sides. Add a little more oil if the rice cakes are too sticky.

4 Add the lap cheong and prawns and stir-fry until the prawns are cooked. Add the soy sauce, dark soy caramel and white pepper, and give it a quick stir to make sure the rice cakes are well coated in the sauce.

5 Push the rice cakes aside and make a clear space in the wok, then add the remaining tablespoon of oil and crack the egg into the oil. Stir to break up the egg with a spatula, then quickly cover it up with rice cakes and let it cook for 10–15 seconds before you start stir-frying again. Add the bean sprouts and garlic chives, then turn the heat off and give everything in the wok a gentle toss to combine. Tip out onto a serving plate and serve with Sriracha chilli sauce.

CHAR kuey teow

3 tablespoons vegetable oil

2 tablespoons garlic, finely chopped

2 or 3 strips of salted radish, rinsed and patted dry, then finely chopped

1 lap cheong (Chinese sausage, see note page 94), thinly sliced

6 raw prawns (shrimp), peeled and deveined

250 g (9 oz) fresh flat rice noodles (see note)

2 tablespoons light soy sauce

2 teaspoons dark soy caramel

pinch of ground white pepper

1 egg

handful of bean sprouts

handful of garlic chives, cut into 5 cm (2 inch) lengths

Sriracha chilli sauce, to serve

1 Heat 2 tablespoons of the vegetable oil in a non-stick wok over high heat, then add the garlic and salted radish and fry until fragrant. Add the lap cheong and prawns and stir-fry for 2 minutes until cooked.

2 Add the rice noodles, then toss to mix everything together. Add the light soy sauce, dark soy caramel and white pepper, and give it a quick stir-fry to make sure all the noodles are now charred and well coated in the sauce.

3 Push the rice noodles aside and make a clear space in the wok, then add the remaining tablespoon of oil and crack the egg into the oil. Stir to break up the egg with the spatula, then quickly cover it up with noodles and let it cook for 10–15 seconds before you start stir-frying again. Add the bean sprouts and garlic chives, turn the heat off, then give everything in the wok a toss to combine. Tip out onto a serving plate and serve with Sriracha chilli sauce.

Note: Fresh flat rice noodles are available in the refrigerated section in Asian grocers or major supermarkets. They are usually sold as a block of noodles in a packet. To loosen the noodles, take them out of the packet and heat them in the microwave for 60 seconds, then dip the noodles in a bowl of lukewarm water. The noodles should now be pliable enough to separate into individual strands. Drain the noodles and let them dry in a colander before cooking.

THIS IS A NOODLE DISH I CAN EAT ALL DAY LONG, FOR BREAKFAST, LUNCH, DINNER OR EVEN SUPPER. CHAR KUEY TEOW, COMMONLY KNOWN AS CKT, IS A HAWKER FOOD INSTITUTION LOVED BY MANY MALAYSIANS. THE SECRET TO A MOUTH-WATERING CKT IS TO MAKE SURE THE WOK IS SMOKING HOT WHEN STIR-FRYING THE NOODLES. THE HIGH HEAT WILL PREVENT THE INGREDIENTS FROM STICKING TO THE WOK AND INEVITABLY BURNING, BUT IT ALSO GIVES THE DISH A NICE CHARRED FLAVOUR, OFTEN REFERRED TO AS THE 'BREATH OF THE WOK'.

300 g (10½ oz/1½ cups)
    jasmine rice, rinsed
    3 times
5 slices of ginger
2 litres (68 fl oz/8 cups)
    water, plus more to top up
4 tablespoons light soy sauce
1 teaspoon sesame oil
1 teaspoon salt
1 teaspoon ground white
    pepper
2 century eggs, peeled and
    roughly chopped (see note)

PORK MINCE BALLS

300 g (10½ oz) minced
    (ground) pork
2 tablespoons light
    soy sauce
2 garlic cloves, finely
    chopped
1 teaspoon sesame oil
1 teaspoon ground white
    pepper
1 egg, beaten
1 tablespoon cornflour
    (cornstarch)

EXTRA CONDIMENTS (FRIED ANCHOVIES WITH PEANUTS)
(optional)
125 ml (4 fl oz/½ cup)
    vegetable oil
100 g (3½ oz/⅓ cup) raw
    peanuts, skins on
60 g (2 oz) ikan bilis (dried
    anchovies)
1 tablespoon caster
    (superfine) sugar

1 Put the rice, ginger and water in a large pot over high heat and bring to the boil. Reduce the heat to low and cook for 30 minutes, or until the rice is mushy, stirring occasionally with a wooden spoon and scraping the base of the pot to make sure no rice sticks to the bottom and burns.

2 Meanwhile, to make the pork mince balls, put all the ingredients into a bowl and mix well. When the congee is about ready, scoop up a tablespoon of pork mixture and drop it into the congee. Repeat until all the mince is used. Stir gently and let the pork balls cook for about 10 minutes in the congee.

3 Season the congee with soy sauce, sesame oil, salt and white pepper. Add the century eggs and stir for 5 minutes. Keep the congee warm on very low heat until ready to serve.

4 To make the extra condiments, heat the vegetable oil in a frying pan over medium heat and fry the peanuts for about 1 minute until golden brown. Strain the oil into a bowl to be reused, and spread the peanuts on a tray lined with paper towel. Pour the oil back into the pan and reheat it. Now fry the anchovies for 2 minutes until crispy and golden. Drain the oil and spread the fried anchovies on the tray with the peanuts. Put the peanuts and anchovies into a bowl and sprinkle with the caster sugar, tossing to mix well. Serve on the side with the congee, perhaps with other accompaniments such as pickled cabbage and radish, and fermented spicy tofu.

Note: Century eggs, or hundred-year eggs, are usually chicken or duck eggs that have been preserved for many months in a mixture of clay, ash, salt and lime, which gives them a dark green, almost black colour, and an odour of sulphur and ammonia from the preserving. They are available from Asian grocers and usually come in a vacuum-sealed packet.

Pork mince balls & CENTURY EGGS CONGEE

THERE'S SOMETHING SO SPECIAL AND COMFORTING ABOUT MUM'S COOKING. WHEN I WAS YOUNG, MY MUM ALWAYS MADE A BIG POT OF RICE CONGEE WHENEVER I FELT ILL AND LOST MY APPETITE. I THINK MANY CHINESE FAMILIES FOLLOW THIS TRADITION, BELIEVING THAT THE LITTLE BOWL OF HUMBLE RICE PORRIDGE IS THE BEST REMEDY TO HEAL THE WEAKENING BODY AND SOUL. STILL TODAY, I MAKE A POT OF THIS CONGEE WHENEVER I FEEL A LITTLE UNDER THE WEATHER, THEN SPEND THE WHOLE DAY BURROWED UNDER THE BLANKET IN FRONT OF THE TV, WITH A BOWL OF THIS COMFORTING CONGEE. IT IS A MUM'S WARM HUG IN A BOWL.

Penang har mee
{PRAWN NOODLE SOUP}

HAR MEE LITERALLY MEANS 'PRAWN NOODLES' IN THE HOKKIEN DIALECT OF CHINESE. IT IS ANOTHER SPECIALTY FROM FUJIAN PROVINCE IN CHINA THAT HAS BEEN MADE FAMOUS IN PENANG, MALAYSIA. THIS IS A GREAT ALTERNATIVE FOR THOSE WHO DON'T LIKE THEIR FOOD TOO HOT (LIKE THE LAKSA), AND YOU CAN ADJUST THE HEAT LEVEL BY ADDING MORE OR LESS OF THE DRIED CHILLI PASTE INTO THE STOCK.

2 tablespoons vegetable oil

3 garlic cloves, finely chopped

3 cm (1¼ inch) piece ginger, peeled and finely chopped

200 g (7 oz) frozen prawn (shrimp) heads (collected from 500 g/ 1 lb 2 oz raw prawns) (see tip)

300 g (10½ oz) cooked fresh prawns (shrimp), peeled and deveined, reserving the heads with the rest

2 litres (68 fl oz/8 cups) water

200 g (7 oz) pork loin medallion

salt, to taste

450 g (1 lb) packet fresh hokkien egg noodles (microwaved in a bowl for 3 minutes to soften)

200 g (7 oz) packet dried rice vermicelli, soaked in warm water for 30 minutes

1 bunch of kangkong (water spinach), washed and cut into 5 cm (2 inch) lengths

2–3 hard-boiled eggs, halved

DRIED CHILLI PASTE

30 g (1 oz) dried red chillies, seeded then soaked in hot water for 30 minutes to soften

180 g (6½ oz) French shallots, peeled

20 dried shrimp, soaked in water for 10 minutes then drained

5 garlic cloves, peeled

2 tablespoons water

125 ml (4 fl oz/½ cup) vegetable oil

2 tablespoons sugar

1 teaspoon salt

1 Heat the vegetable oil in a wok and fry the garlic and ginger for 1 minute until fragrant, then add the prawn heads and cook until they turn pink and lightly browned. Pour in 250 ml (8½ fl oz/1 cup) water to deglaze the wok, then tip all the cooked prawn heads and the juice into a food processor. Process into a rough purée.

2 Fill a large stockpot with 2 litres (68 fl oz/ 8 cups) water, add the prawn purée and bring to the boil over high heat. Lower the heat to medium, then cook the pork loin in the stock for 5 minutes. Remove and set aside to cool, then slice into thin strips.

3 Continue to simmer the stock for another 45 minutes over low heat, then strain it into another pot through a fine sieve, discarding the solids. Season to taste, and keep the stock warm on a very low heat.

4 Meanwhile, to make the chilli paste, put the chillies, shallots, dried shrimp, garlic and water in a food processor and process to a fine paste. Heat the vegetable oil in a wok over medium heat, and fry the chilli paste for about 10 minutes, or until it is fragrant and turns a darker brown. Season with the sugar and salt, then remove from the heat and pour into a bowl to cool. Add 2 tablespoons of the chilli paste to the prawn stock, reserving the rest to use as a condiment for serving.

5 Fill another pot with water and bring to a vigorous rolling boil. For each serve, put about 80 g (3 oz) hokkien noodles, 50 g (2 oz) rice vermicelli and a handful of kangkong in a wire mesh sieve, then dunk it into the water and scald the noodles for 30 seconds. Drain and shake off any excess water, then transfer into a serving bowl. Top with a couple of prawns, some slices of pork and half an egg, then ladle the hot prawn stock over the top. Serve with extra chilli paste, to add to the soup as desired.

Tip: To prepare a prawn stock that has the rich depth of flavour needed for this dish, it's a good idea to start saving raw prawn heads every time you cook a prawn dish, and keep them in the freezer in a zip-lock bag.

Curry LAKSA

SERVES 6

2 litres (68 fl oz/8 cups) water

500 g (1 lb 2 oz) raw prawns (shrimp), peeled and deveined, tails left on (reserve the prawn heads)

1 boneless, skinless chicken breast

125 ml (4 fl oz/½ cup) vegetable oil

400 ml (13 fl oz) tinned coconut cream

salt, to taste

200 g (7 oz) packet fried tofu puffs, halved

450 g (1 lb) packet fresh hokkien egg noodles, microwaved in a bowl for 3 minutes to soften

200 g (7 oz) packet dried rice vermicelli, soaked in warm water for 10 minutes then drained

200 g (7 oz) bean sprouts

3 hard-boiled eggs, halved

100 g (3½ oz) fish cake, thinly sliced (see note page 61)

handful of mint leaves

handful of Vietnamese coriander (cilantro) (see note)

LAKSA PASTE

5 cm (2 inch) piece galangal, peeled and chopped

5 cm (2 inch) piece turmeric, peeled and chopped (or 1 tablespoon ground powder)

250 g (9 oz) French shallots, peeled

10 garlic cloves, chopped

20 dried red chillies, seeded then soaked in hot water for 30 minutes to soften (use less chillies if you don't like it too hot)

6 large fresh red chillies, seeded and chopped

10 candlenuts, roasted (see note page 272)

50 g (2 oz) dried shrimp, soaked in hot water for 10 minutes then drained

2 tablespoons belachan (dried shrimp paste), toasted

2 lemongrass stalks, white part only, chopped

CURRY LAKSA IS A COCONUT-BASED CURRY NOODLE SOUP ALSO KNOWN IN MALAYSIA AS LAKSA LEMAK OR CURRY MEE. IT IS SOMETIMES REFERRED TO SIMPLY AS 'LAKSA'. THIS DISH IS A PERFECT WINTER WARMER — SLURP UP THE STEAMING HOT NOODLES ALONG WITH THE RICH AND SPICY COCONUT CURRY BROTH. YOU HAVEN'T FULLY ENJOYED THIS DISH IF THERE AREN'T ANY BEADS OF PERSPIRATION ON YOUR FOREHEAD AND CHILLI OIL SPLASHES ON YOUR SHIRT!

1 Pour the water into a large stockpot and bring to the boil, then turn the heat down to a simmer, add the chicken and let it cook in the hot water for 20 minutes. Remove the chicken, set aside to cool, then shred the chicken into small pieces.

2 Add the prawn heads to the pot and bring to the boil again. Reduce the heat to medium–low and simmer for 30 minutes. Scoop out the heads and discard them.

3 Meanwhile, put all the laksa paste ingredients in a food processor, and process to a fine paste.

4 Heat the vegetable oil in a frying pan over medium heat and fry the laksa paste for about 15–20 minutes. The paste should be dark brown and a layer of red oil will separate from the spices. Reserve a few tablespoons for serving later.

5 Add the cooked laksa paste to the stock, stirring to mix well. Pour in the coconut cream and bring to the boil. Season with salt, add the fried tofu puffs, then lower the heat and let the soup simmer until ready to serve.

6 Half fill another large pot with water and bring to the boil. For each serve, grab a handful each of hokkien noodles and rice vermicelli, and a few prawns. Put them into a wire mesh strainer or a sieve and dunk the noodles and prawns into the hot water for 1 minute. Add a handful of bean sprouts to the strainer and blanch for a further 15 seconds, drain and shake off any excess water, then transfer to a serving bowl. Repeat to make another 5 serves. Top each bowl of noodles with half an egg, a few slices of fish cake and some shredded chicken, then ladle the hot laksa broth along with a few tofu puffs over the top. Garnish with mint leaves and Vietnamese coriander. Serve with the reserved laksa paste on the side, to add to the soup as desired.

Note: Vietnamese coriander (cilantro) is also known as Vietnamese mint or laksa leaf, and can be found in Asian grocers. It has a subtle heat as well as the coriander flavour. You can substitute it with common coriander (cilantro) leaves.

Assam laksa

Curry laksa

ASSAM LAKSA
{SPICY & SOUR *fish stock* LAKSA}

LAKSAS TEND TO BE QUITE RICH AND HEAVY, SO IF YOU ARE LOOKING FOR A LIGHTER VERSION THEN THIS NOODLE DISH IN A SOUR FISH-BASED BROTH MIGHT BE JUST WHAT YOU'RE LOOKING FOR. THE BROTH HAS A DISTINCTIVE SPICY PIQUANT FLAVOUR, SOURED WITH TAMARIND PULP AND TAMARIND PEEL, AND THE FISHY AROMA OF MACKEREL IS DELICIOUSLY ADDICTIVE. ASSAM LAKSA IS ALSO KNOWN AS PENANG LAKSA, AND MANY PEOPLE WOULD AGREE THAT NO VISIT TO PENANG IS COMPLETE WITHOUT EATING THIS FAMOUS AND MUCH-LOVED LOCAL DELICACY.

500 g (1 lb 2 oz) mackerel fillets
   (see notes)
2 litres (68 fl oz/8 cups) water
3–4 pieces dried tamarind peel
   (see notes)
110 g (3¾ oz) tamarind purée
3 sprigs Vietnamese coriander
   (cilantro), plus extra for garnish
2 tablespoons har go (prawn paste), plus
   extra to serve (see notes)
1 tablespoon salt, or to taste
2 tablespoons sugar, or to taste
600 g (1 lb 5 oz) packet fresh lai fun
   noodles (see notes), microwaved in a
   bowl for 2 minutes to soften
2 tablespoons vegetable oil
100 g (3½ oz) peeled fresh pineapple,
   finely diced
1 large green cucumber, halved and
   seeded, julienned into thin strips
1 red onion, thinly sliced
handful of mint leaves,
   for garnish

SPICE PASTE

200 g (7 oz) French shallots, peeled
2 lemongrass stalks, white part only,
   finely chopped
5 large fresh red chillies
5 g (⅛ oz) dried red chillies (10–12), seeded
   then soaked in hot water for 30 minutes
   until softened, then drained
40 g (1½ oz) belachan (dried shrimp paste)

MAKES
6

1 Put the mackerel on a plate and place inside a steamer. Cover with the lid and place the steamer over a wok or saucepan of simmering water. Steam the fish for 10 minutes, or until cooked. Remove and set aside to cool, then flake the fish into tiny pieces, taking care to remove all the bones.

2 Put all the spice paste ingredients into a food processor, and process into a fine paste.

3 Pour the water into a large pot. Add the tamarind peel and purée, sprigs of Vietnamese coriander and the spice paste, and bring to the boil. Add two-thirds of the flaked fish to the stock, then reduce the heat to low and simmer for 1 hour. Season with the har go, and the salt and sugar, to taste.

4 Half fill another large pot with water and bring to the boil. Scald the softened noodles for 30 seconds, strain using a colander, then rinse under cold water. Drizzle with the oil and give the noodles a stir so they don't stick in a clump.

5 To serve, place a handful of noodles in a serving bowl, top with a small handful of flaked fish, some pineapple, cucumber and onion. Ladle hot laksa soup over the noodles and the toppings. Garnish with Vietnamese coriander and mint leaves, and serve with extra har go on the side.

Notes: If using whole mackerel fish, make sure to clean, gut and fillet the fish first before steaming, which will save you the hassle of trying to look for all the tiny little bones when flaking the fish. Mackerel can be substituted with any oily fish with a strong fishy flavour, such as wolf herring, sardines or maybe even sea mullet.

Tamarind peel (called assam in Malay) is actually a small yellow fruit and not related to the tamarind pods that we are more familiar with. It is more sour than tamarind pulp with not much flavour, hence it is only used as a souring agent in cooking. Tamarind peel is available from Asian grocers, but if you can't find it, just omit it from the recipe — no biggie.

Prawn paste (or har go in Chinese) is a thick prawn sauce that is dark brown, almost black in colour (don't confuse it with the pungent belachan dried shrimp paste). It is sweetened and can be eaten straight away, and is typically used as a dressing in a fruit salad called rojak. It is available from Asian grocers.

Lai fun noodles, or laksa noodles, are thick round rice noodles found in Asian grocers. They can be substituted with dried Vietnamese bun bo Hue noodles. If using dried bun bo Hue noodles, simply cook the noodles in boiling water for 20 minutes, then rinse in cold water and drizzle with oil to prevent them sticking.

CHAPTER 6

Life is like a box of chocolates ❖ POPCORN & SALTED CARAMEL MACARONS ❖ Fudgy macadamia & peanut butter brownies ❖ PANDAN KAYA LAMINGTON ❖ Peach frangipane tart ❖ LEMON! ❖ Dear I miss you (tiramisu deconstructed) ❖ BILLY'S FAMOUS ROCKY ROAD ❖ You saucy thing, you! ❖ CHEWIE WOOKIE CHOC CHIP COOKIE ❖ Lemon myrtle delicious ❖ TARTS — SWEET PASTRY TART CASES; PASSIONFRUIT MERINGUE; MACADAMIA & SALTED CARAMEL; NO-BAKE KEY LIME; CHILLI CHOCOLATE GANACHE; CHOCOLATE & PEANUT BUTTER ❖ Flourless chocolate cake with morello cherries ❖ PETE'S MUM'S FAIL-PROOF TREACLE PUDDING ❖ Ondeh ondeh (coconut glutinous rice balls) ❖ VEGEMITE CHEESECAKE ❖ Ice cream — coconut; avocado; peanut butter; matcha; gingerbread ❖ CHOCOLATE & SALTED CARAMEL POTS DE CRÈME

THERE'S NO DENYING THAT THIS IS MY FAVOURITE CHAPTER IN THE BOOK. FROM HOME-BAKED SWEET TREATS TO FINE DINING AND BEAUTIFULLY PRESENTED DESSERTS, THESE RECIPES WILL KEEP YOU IRRESISTIBLY SWEET ALL YEAR ROUND.

Life IS LIKE a box of CHOCOLATES

CHOCOLATE BROWNIE (BOTTOM LAYER)

1 egg

100 g (3½ oz) caster (superfine) sugar

200 g (7 oz) dark chocolate (65%)

60 g (2 oz) unsalted butter, melted

30 g (1 oz/¼ cup) plain (all-purpose) flour

20 g (¾ oz) unsweetened cocoa powder

½ teaspoon baking powder

50 g (2 oz) macadamia nuts, toasted then roughly chopped

CHOCOLATE GANACHE (MIDDLE LAYER)

300 g (10½ oz) dark chocolate (65%), roughly chopped

375 ml (13 fl oz/1½ cups) thickened (whipping) cream (35% fat)

110 g (3¾ oz/½ cup) caster (superfine) sugar

a box of assorted chocolates (about 16–20)

CHOCOLATE GLAZE (TOP LAYER)

100 g (3½ oz) dark chocolate (65%), roughly chopped

150 ml (5 fl oz) water

55 g (2 oz/¼ cup) caster (superfine) sugar

55 g (2 oz) unsweetened cocoa powder

100 ml (3½ fl oz) thickened (whipping) cream (35% fat)

SERVES
12

I AM A SELF-CONFESSED CHOCOHOLIC AND PROBABLY THE ONLY ONE MAD ENOUGH TO CREATE THIS 100 PER CENT SHEER CHOCOLATE INDULGENCE. BUT IS IT WORTH IT? YOU BETCHA! WHAT MAKES THIS CAKE SO UNIQUE AND FUN TO EAT IS THE LITTLE SURPRISES OF RANDOM CHOCOLATES HIDDEN INSIDE — JUST LIKE A BOX OF CHOCOLATES, YOU NEVER KNOW WHAT YOU'RE GOING TO GET UNTIL YOU BITE INTO IT!

1 First, make the chocolate brownie layer. Preheat the oven to 180°C (350°F). Grease a 20 cm (8 inch) square baking tin, then line the base and sides with baking paper.

2 Put the egg and sugar in a mixing bowl and whisk until thick and pale. Melt the chocolate in a large heatproof bowl over a saucepan of simmering water over low heat. Do not let the water touch the base of the bowl. Remove the bowl from the heat, stir in the melted butter, then fold in the sugar and egg mixture.

3 Sift the flour, cocoa powder and baking powder into the egg mixture, then fold everything together until well combined. Add the macadamias and mix well, then pour the mixture into the prepared tin. Spread the mixture with a palette knife to fill all the corners, and smooth the surface. Bake the brownie for 12 minutes, or until it is just cooked but still a little soft in the middle. Remove from the oven and leave to cool, then transfer to the refrigerator to set for at least 1 hour, or overnight.

4 Meanwhile, make the chocolate ganache. Put the chopped chocolate in a large mixing bowl and set aside. Heat the cream and sugar in a saucepan over medium heat and bring to the boiling. Quickly remove the pan from the heat and pour the hot cream mixture into the chocolate. Let the chocolate soften for 2 minutes, then use a spatula to slowly stir the mixture from the centre in small circles, gradually increasing the stirring strokes until all the chocolate has melted. Set aside to cool to room temperature.

5 Take the brownie out of the refrigerator and randomly place the assorted chocolates on top of the brownie. Once the chocolate ganache has cooled down, pour it all over the brownie in the tin, to cover all the chocolates. Refrigerate again to set for at least 4 hours, or ideally overnight.

6 To make the chocolate glaze, put the chopped chocolate in a heatproof bowl. Heat the water and sugar in a small saucepan over medium heat, stirring until the sugar has dissolved. Whisk in the cocoa powder and cream, bring to the boil, then immediately turn the heat down to low and simmer for 10 minutes. Remove from the heat and pour the hot liquid onto the chocolate in the bowl. Let the chocolate soften for a minute, then stir the mixture until the chocolate has melted. Pass the chocolate mixture through a fine sieve and leave to cool to room temperature.

7 Take the chocolate out of the refrigerator. Dip the baking tin in warm water for 10 seconds, then remove the chocolate from the tin and set it on a wire rack over a baking tray. Pour the chocolate glaze over the top and let it drip over the sides, smoothing the surface with a palette knife if necessary. Carefully return the whole chocolate masterpiece back to the refrigerator to set for at least 1 hour.

8 Take the chocolate out of the refrigerator 30 minutes before serving. Use a kitchen blowtorch to gently reheat the chocolate glaze to make it glossy again. Slice the cake into small pieces (be warned, it is very rich!) with a hot, wet knife by dipping the knife in hot water for 10–15 seconds.

POPCORN & SALTED CARAMEL MACARONS

AFTER COUNTLESS ATTEMPTS AND MANY FAILURES, THIS RECIPE IS MY FORMULA FOR MACARON SUCCESS. HAVING SAID THAT, I WON'T GUARANTEE THIS WILL ALWAYS WORK FOR EVERYONE. THERE ARE MANY REASONS WHY YOUR MACARONS MIGHT FLOP, INCLUDING HOW YOU FOLD THE BATTER AND THE TEMPERAMENT OF YOUR OVEN. THUS, MY ADVICE IS: PRACTISE, PRACTISE, PRACTISE!

110 g (3¾ oz) almond meal (ground almonds)

200 g (7 oz) icing (confectioners') sugar

3 tablespoons water

60 g (2 oz) caster (superfine) sugar

90 g (3 oz) egg whites (about 3 egg whites), at room temperature

10 g (½ oz/½ cup) popcorn, blitzed while still warm

4 tablespoons Salted caramel (page 246)

BUTTERCREAM

100 g (3½ oz) unsalted butter, softened

200 g (7 oz) icing (confectioners') sugar

4 tablespoons Salted caramel (page 246)

1 Put the almond meal and icing sugar into a food processor, process the mixture for 30 seconds, scrape down the side, then process again for another 30 seconds. Sieve the mixture into a bowl and set aside.

2 Put the water and sugar in a small saucepan and bring to the boil. Keep an eye on the temperature of the sugar syrup by using a sugar thermometer. Once the temperature reaches 110°C (230°F), start whisking the egg whites using an electric stand mixer until soft peaks form. When the temperature reaches 115°C (240°F), remove the sugar syrup from the heat, and slowly pour the syrup in a steady stream down the side of the mixing bowl into the egg whites. Increase the speed and whisk the meringue for another 10 minutes until it cools down. It should be smooth and glossy.

3 Remove the bowl of meringue from the mixer. Add half the almond mixture and fold together until well combined, then fold in the remaining almond mixture in two batches. This technique is known as *macaronage* and is crucial for perfect macarons; the batter should be thick and have a lava-like consistency.

Scrape the mixture into a piping bag with an 8 mm (⅜ inch) round tip.

4 Line a baking tray with baking paper. Pipe the macaron batter onto the tray, about 4 cm (1½ inches) in diameter. Once the tray is filled, pick up the tray and give it a gentle tap on the kitchen bench to smooth the top. Sprinkle with the popcorn flakes and set aside for 1 hour to set.

5 Preheat the oven to 140°C (275°F). Place the macarons in the oven and bake for 17–20 minutes. Remove from the oven and cool on the tray for 10 minutes, then peel the macaron shells off the baking paper and place them on a wire rack. If the shells stick to the paper, return the tray to the oven and bake for another 10 minutes.

6 To make the buttercream, beat the butter until pale and creamy. Add the icing sugar, 1 tablespoon at a time, beating until incorporated. Add the salted caramel and beat until combined. Scrape the buttercream into a piping bag. Pipe a dollop of buttercream on the flat side of one macaron shell, top with another shell, and press it down gently. Repeat until all the macaron shells are filled.

FUDGY MACADAMIA & PEANUT BUTTER BROWNIES

50 g (2 oz/⅓ cup) plain (all-purpose) flour
40 g (1½ oz/⅓ cup) unsweetened cocoa powder, plus extra for dusting
pinch of salt

300 g (10½ oz) dark chocolate (65%), roughly chopped
150 g (5 oz) unsalted butter, cut into cubes
300 g (10½ oz/1⅓ cups firmly packed) light brown sugar

4 eggs
125 g (4 oz/½ cup) sour cream
100 g (3½ oz) macadamia nuts
12 tablespoons peanut butter

1 Preheat the oven to 180°C (350°F). Grease a 20 × 30 × 4 cm (8 × 12 × 1½ inch) rectangular baking tin, then line the base and sides with baking paper. Sift the flour, cocoa and salt into a bowl and set aside.

2 Melt the chocolate and butter in a heatproof bowl over a saucepan of simmering water. Do not let the water touch the base of the bowl. Stir occasionally until the chocolate and butter have melted, then remove the pan from the heat and set aside to cool for 10 minutes.

3 Stir the brown sugar into the chocolate, then add the eggs, one at a time, stirring well after each addition. Add the flour mixture, stir to combine, then add the sour cream and macadamia nuts and stir to mix well.

4 Pour the mixture into the tin, spreading it with a palette knife to fill all the corners and to smooth the surface. Using a tablespoon, place 12 dollops of peanut butter evenly over the mixture, then wet your index finger with water and gently poke the peanut butter and bury it in the chocolate mixture. Use the palette knife to smooth out the surface again.

5 Bake the brownies for 30 minutes, or until just set. Remove and allow to cool completely. Dust with extra cocoa powder and slice into 5 cm (2 inch) squares.

MAKES
20

IT WAS THE HUMBLE CHOCOLATE BROWNIE THAT FIRST SPARKED MY PASSION FOR BAKING. IF YOU HAVE A SWEET TOOTH LIKE ME AND HAVE ALWAYS WANTED TO LEARN HOW TO MAKE SWEET TREATS, THEN THIS RECIPE IS A GOOD KICK-START FOR BEGINNERS. IT IS SUPER SIMPLE AND FAST TO MAKE, AND GREAT TO HAVE ON STANDBY FOR WHEN YOU HAVE UNEXPECTED GUESTS OR ARE SIMPLY CRAVING SOMETHING SWEET. I LOVE THE CONTRAST OF THE CRUNCHY MACADAMIAS AGAINST THE FUDGY CAKE, AND THE PEANUT BUTTER IS A NAUGHTY TOUCH FOR THAT ULTIMATE INDULGENCE.

Pandan kaya LAMINGTON

MAKES 15

50 g (2 oz) cornflour (cornstarch)
75 g (2½ oz/½ cup) plain (all-purpose) flour
50 g (2 oz/⅓ cup) self-raising flour
6 eggs
150 g (5 oz/⅔ cup) caster (superfine) sugar
1 teaspoon pandan essence
125 ml (4 fl oz/½ cup) Kaya jam (page 93)
180 g (6½ oz/2 cups) desiccated coconut

CHOCOLATE SAUCE
150 ml (5 fl oz) water
175 g (6 oz/¾ cup) caster (superfine) sugar
50 g (2 oz) unsweetened cocoa powder
250 ml (8½ fl oz/1 cup) thickened (whipping)
   cream (35% fat)
100 g (3½ oz) dark chocolate (65%), chopped

1 Preheat the oven to 180°C (350°F). Grease two rectangular 15 × 20 cm (6 × 8 inch) cake tins and line with baking paper. Triple sift the cornflour, plain flour and self-raising flour into a bowl, then set aside.

2 Using an electric mixer on high speed, whisk the eggs for 10 minutes until thick and frothy. Then gradually add the sugar, whisking constantly until the mixture has tripled in volume. Using a metal spoon, fold one-third of the egg mixture and the pandan essence into the flour, making sure it is well incorporated. Then fold in the rest of the egg mixture in two batches — be extremely gentle and try not to knock too much air out of the batter. Divide the cake mixture evenly between the two tins.

3 Bake in the oven for 20–25 minutes. The cakes are ready when a skewer inserted into the centre of the cake comes out clean. Turn off the oven, but leave the cakes in the oven for 10 minutes, then remove and leave to cool in the tins for 10 minutes before turning out onto a wire rack to cool completely.

4 Spread a layer of kaya jam on the flat side of one of the sponge cakes, then sandwich with the other one over the top.

5 To make the chocolate sauce, put the water, sugar and cocoa in a small saucepan and bring to the boil. Reduce the heat and simmer for 10 minutes, then add the cream and bring it back up to boiling point. Put the chopped chocolate in a heatproof bowl, then pour the hot cocoa mixture over the chocolate. Let the chocolate soften for a minute, then stir until the chocolate has melted. Set the chocolate sauce aside until it is cool enough for coating.

6 Have the bowl of chocolate sauce, a bowl of desiccated coconut and a wire rack over a baking tray ready. Cut the cake into fifteen 5 cm (2 inch) cubes. Using two forks, dip the cake into the chocolate sauce, then drop it in the bowl of coconut. Sprinkle the cake with coconut and then roll it around until it is well coated. Repeat for all the cakes. Place the lamingtons on the wire rack to set for 1 hour before serving.

AFTER LIVING IN AUSTRALIA FOR 10 YEARS, I FINALLY
BECAME A CITIZEN IN 2007. OTHER THAN RECEIVING A
CERTIFICATE AND A WATTLE TREE, I WAS GIVEN THREE
OTHER ITEMS FROM FRIENDS THAT HAVE ENCOURAGED
MY PASSION IN COOKING: A CWA COOKBOOK, A MEAT
PIE, AND A LAMINGTON (WHICH I DEVOURED AT THE
CEREMONY). WHILE I DO CALL AUSTRALIA HOME,
A PART OF ME STILL BELONGS TO MALAYSIA. THUS,
THIS PANDAN KAYA LAMINGTON WAS BORN.

3 ripe peaches, halved,
stones removed, then
sliced into 8 thin wedges

4 tablespoons peach or
apricot jam, for glazing

SOUR CREAM PASTRY
125 g (4 oz) chilled unsalted
butter, cut into small
cubes

150 g (5 oz/1 cup) plain
(all-purpose) flour, plus
extra for dusting

65 g ($2\frac{1}{4}$ oz/$\frac{1}{4}$ cup) sour
cream

FRANGIPANE
120 g (4 oz) unsalted butter

110 g ($3\frac{3}{4}$ oz/$\frac{1}{2}$ cup) caster
(superfine) sugar

2 eggs

2 tablespoons brandy

1 teaspoon finely grated
lemon zest

120 g (4 oz/$1\frac{1}{4}$ cups) almond
meal (ground almonds)

30 g (1 oz/$\frac{1}{4}$ cup) plain
(all-purpose) flour

1 To make the sour cream pastry, put the butter and flour
in a food processor and pulse in 2-second bursts until the
mixture resembles breadcrumbs. Add the sour cream and
pulse again until it forms a dough. Gather the dough into a
clump, then use the palm of your hand to gently flatten it into
a flat disc, about 2 cm ($\frac{3}{4}$ inch) thick. Cover the dough in plastic
wrap and leave to rest in the refrigerator for 20–25 minutes.

2 Transfer the chilled dough to a lightly floured surface.
Using a rolling pin, roll the dough out until it is 5 mm
($\frac{1}{4}$ inch) thick and about 30 cm (12 inches) in diameter. Gently
pick up one end of the pastry and roll onto the rolling pin,
then drape the pastry over a 23 cm (9 inch) tart tin with a
removable base. Line the base and side of the tart tin with the
pastry, trim off the excess pastry hanging over the edges, then
chill the pastry case in the refrigerator for 20 minutes.

3 To blind bake, preheat the oven to 200°C (400°F). Lightly
prick the tart base all over with a fork, line the pastry case
with baking paper, then fill the tin with pastry weights, rice
or dried beans. Blind bake the pastry case for 15 minutes, then
remove the baking paper and weights, put the tart case back
in the oven and bake for another 10 minutes until the pastry
is golden brown. Set aside to cool.

4 To make the frangipane, beat the butter and sugar using
an electric mixer until pale and creamy. Add the eggs,
one at a time, and whisk into the mixture on low speed until
combined. With the mixer still running, add the brandy and

ONE OF MY COOKING IDOLS HAS TO BE MAGGIE BEER. I WAS HONOURED TO MEET MAGGIE
ON 'MASTERCHEF', EVEN THOUGH SHE WAS EVIL ENOUGH TO SET AN EXTREMELY DIFFICULT
CHALLENGE FOR US! BUT ALL IS FORGIVEN, AS I HAVE LEARNED SO MUCH FROM MAGGIE, AND
I HAVE HER TO THANK FOR THIS FANTASTIC SOUR CREAM PASTRY RECIPE. THE SOUR CREAM
MAKES THE PASTRY A LITTLE TRICKY TO HANDLE ON WARMER DAYS, SO TAKE YOUR TIME
AND MAKE SURE IT RESTS LONGER IN THE FRIDGE SO IT IS FIRMER AND EASIER TO HANDLE.

Peach frangipane tart

lemon zest, then the almond meal and flour. You will have to stop the mixer a few times to scrape down the bowl, then whisk again to make sure everything is well incorporated.

5 Reduce the oven to 180°C (350°F). Fill the tart case with the frangipane and spread it evenly using a palette knife. Cover the frangipane with the peach slices. Place the tart on a baking tray and bake for 25 minutes, or until a skewer inserted in the centre of the tart comes out clean. Remove from the oven and set aside to cool.

6 Melt the jam in a small saucepan over low heat, then glaze the top of the tart with the jam sauce.

SERVES

8

TO

10

Lemon!

LEMON IS ONE OF THE MOST VERSATILE CITRUS FRUITS, AND THIS DESSERT IS DESIGNED TO ALLOW THE FLAVOUR OF THIS BEAUTIFUL YELLOW FRUIT TO SPEAK FOR ITSELF.

LEMON CURD

2 eggs
2 egg yolks
150 g (5 oz/⅔ cup) caster (superfine) sugar
finely grated zest of 2 lemons
juice of 2 lemons
100 g (3½ oz) chilled unsalted butter, cut into 1 cm (½ inch) cubes

MERINGUE BUTTONS

200 g (7 oz) caster (superfine) sugar
3 egg whites (90 g/3 oz)

LEMON SPONGE

225 g (8 oz/1½ cups) self-raising flour
2 tablespoons cornflour (cornstarch)
125 g (4 oz) unsalted butter, softened
finely grated zest of 1 lemon
150 g (5 oz/⅔ cup) caster (superfine) sugar
2 eggs, separated
170 ml (6 fl oz/⅔ cup) full-cream milk
juice of ½ lemon

SOFT LEMON MERINGUE

60 g (2 oz) caster (superfine) sugar
juice of ½ lemon
30 ml (1 fl oz) water
3 egg whites (90 g/3 oz)

Sweet sable crumbs (page 237)
Coconut ice cream (page 260), to serve

1 To make the lemon curd, whisk the eggs, egg yolks and sugar in a saucepan until smooth. Whisk in the lemon zest and juice, then place the pan over low heat, stirring continuously until the mixture is thick enough to coat the back of a spatula. Add the butter, a few cubes at a time, whisking until the butter has melted before adding more. Strain into a squeeze bottle. Cool, then seal and store in the refrigerator for up to 2 weeks.

2 To make the meringue buttons, preheat the oven to 100°C (200°F). Line a baking tray with baking paper. Put the sugar and egg whites in the bowl of an electric stand mixer. Place the bowl over a saucepan of simmering water over low heat. Do not let the water touch the base of the bowl. Whisk the mixture until it reaches 60°C (140°F) on a sugar thermometer. Remove from the heat, then whisk the hot mixture using the electric mixer for 10 minutes until the meringue is stiff and glossy and has doubled in volume. Scrape the meringue into a piping bag with 1 cm ($\frac{1}{2}$ inch) round tip, and pipe about 20 meringue buttons about the size of a 50-cent coin onto the tray. Bake for $2\frac{1}{2}$ hours, or until crispy and dry. Leave to cool in the oven, then store in an airtight container.

3 To make the lemon sponge, preheat the oven to 180°C (350°F). Grease a 20 cm (8 inch) square cake tin and line it with baking paper. Sift the flour and cornflour together and set aside. Beat the butter, lemon zest and sugar using an electric mixer on high speed until pale and creamy. Turn the speed to low and gradually beat in the egg yolks, one at a time, then add the milk, lemon juice and sifted flour, beating until just combined, taking care that you don't overwork the mixture.

4 In a clean bowl, whisk the egg whites until soft peaks form, then, in 3 batches, gently fold the meringue into the cake mixture. Pour into the cake tin and bake for 30 minutes, or until a skewer inserted into the centre of the cake comes out clean. Remove from the oven, cool a little in the tin, then transfer to a wire rack to cool completely.

5 To make the soft lemon meringue, put the sugar, lemon juice and water in a saucepan over medium–high heat and bring to the boil without stirring. When the sugar syrup reaches 110°C (230°F), whisk the egg whites in an electric stand mixer on medium–high speed until soft peaks form. Once the sugar syrup reaches 115°C (240°F), remove the pan from the heat. Slow down the speed of the mixer, then pour the hot syrup in a steady stream down the side of the bowl, letting it slowly drip into the meringue. Don't let any syrup catch on the whisk, or it will crystallise and you will have to start again. Turn the speed back to medium–high and whisk the meringue for about 10 minutes until it has doubled in volume and is stiff and glossy. Scrape the meringue into a piping bag with a 1 cm ($\frac{1}{2}$ inch) round tip.

6 To serve, pipe a big dollop of the lemon meringue on the plate and drag to the edge in one swift motion. Use a kitchen blowtorch to lightly brown the meringue. Cut the lemon sponge into a 3 × 10 cm ($1\frac{1}{4}$ × 4 inch) rectangle and place on top of the meringue. Pipe a few dollops of lemon curd on the plate. Add a heaped teaspoon of sable crumbs next to the sponge, and place a quenelle of coconut ice cream on top. Sprinkle with extra crumbs all over and garnish with a few meringue buttons.

Dear I miss you
{TIRAMISU DECONSTRUCTED}

COFFEE SPONGE

3 eggs

1 egg yolk

45 g (1½ oz) caster (superfine) sugar

25 g (1 oz) plain (all-purpose) flour

2 tablespoons espresso coffee granules

MASCARPONE FOAM

125 g (4 oz) mascarpone

3 tablespoons thickened (whipping) cream (35% fat)

3 tablespoons plain yoghurt

3 tablespoons chilled water

1 teaspoon honey

25 g (1 oz) caster (superfine) sugar

CHOCOLATE TWIGS

25 g (1 oz) chilled butter, cut into cubes

35 g (1¼ oz/¼ cup) plain (all-purpose) flour, plus extra for dusting

30 g (1 oz/¼ cup) Dutch-process unsweetened cocoa powder

2 tablespoons caster (superfine) sugar

2 tablespoons chilled water

CHOCOLATE AMARETTO GANACHE

200 g (7 oz) dark chocolate (70%), roughly chopped

75 g (2½ oz/⅓ cup) caster (superfine) sugar

125 ml (4 fl oz/½ cup) thickened (whipping) cream (35% fat)

pinch of salt

4 tablespoons amaretto liqueur

40 g (1½ oz/½ cup) chocolate-coated popping candy (see notes)

recipe over →

THIS IS THE DECONSTRUCTED TIRAMISU I CAME UP WITH WHEN I WAS ON 'MASTERCHEF'. I HAD HOPED TO CREATE THIS DESSERT FOR ONE OF THE CHALLENGES, SO I COULD DEDICATE IT TO MY PARTNER, PETE (TIRAMISU IS HIS FAVOURITE DESSERT). SADLY, I NEVER HAD THE CHANCE TO DO SO, AS I WAS ELIMINATED FROM THE COMPETITION. BUT LUCK HAS COME MY WAY, AND I NOW HAVE THE OPPORTUNITY TO PUBLISH THE RECIPE IN THIS COOKBOOK! IT IS A COMPLEX DESSERT AND SPECIAL EQUIPMENT IS REQUIRED FOR SOME OF THE COMPONENTS, BUT EVERY TIME I MAKE THIS FOR HIM, THE LOOK ON HIS FACE MAKES ALL THE HARD WORK WORTHWHILE. SO, IS THERE SOMEONE IN YOUR LIFE THAT YOU REALLY MISS?

1 To make the coffee sponge, put all the ingredients in a food processor and blitz for 2 minutes until well combined. Pour the mixture into a siphon gun and charge with 3 canisters (see notes). Put in the refrigerator to rest for 1 hour.

2 Meanwhile, to make the mascarpone foam, beat the mascarpone using an electric mixer on high speed until soft. Turn the speed to low and then add the remaining ingredients, beating until well combined. Pour the mixture into another siphon gun and charge with 2 canisters. Transfer to the refrigerator.

3 To make the chocolate twigs (these can be made a day in advance), put the butter, flour, cocoa and sugar in a mixing bowl. Using your fingers, rub the butter into the flour until it forms a breadcrumb-like texture. Add the water and stir with a fork until it forms a dough.

4 Preheat the oven to 180°C (350°F). Grease a baking tray and line with baking paper. Dust your hands with flour, then take a small piece of the dough (3–4 g/$\frac{1}{8}$ oz, about the size of a grape) and place it on a lightly floured surface. Roll the dough back and forth to form a rope — roll it as long and as thinly as possible; it should be about 2 mm ($\frac{1}{16}$ inch) thick. Carefully transfer the dough twig to the baking tray and repeat the process until half the dough is used.

5 For the remaining half, simply use a rolling pin to roll the dough into one 2 mm ($\frac{1}{8}$ inch) thick disc, then place it on the same baking tray. Bake the chocolate twigs and disc for 10 minutes, the remove and set aside to cool. Keep the twigs in a container for later use. Put the chocolate disc in a food processor and blitz into fine crumbs. Set aside for later use.

6 To make the chocolate amaretto ganache, put the chopped chocolate in a heatproof bowl and set aside. Heat the sugar and cream in a small saucepan over medium–high until just starting to boil. Remove from the heat and pour the hot mixture over the chocolate. Let the chocolate soften for 30 seconds, then stir the mixture until the chocolate has melted. Sprinkle with salt, add the amaretto and stir well, then transfer to the refrigerator to set for at least 1 hour.

7 To cook the coffee sponge, first prepare 4 paper cups by using a knife to make a small slit in the bottom of each cup. Take the siphon gun with the coffee sponge mixture out of the refrigerator and shake vigorously. Pipe the coffee foam into each cup, filling it about two-thirds full. Place the cups in the microwave, set the microwave power to 70 per cent, and cook the sponge for 40 seconds. Remove the sponge cakes from the microwave, taking care as they are very hot, run a knife around the side of the cup, then tip the sponge cake out onto a wire rack to cool. Once the sponge is cool enough to handle, use your fingers to break it into smaller pieces in different shapes and sizes.

8 To serve, place a trail of chocolate crumbs on the plate, place a quenelle of chocolate amaretto ganache in the centre, then the coffee sponge pieces on each side. Shake the mascarpone in the siphon gun vigorously and pipe mascarpone foam onto the plate, then sprinkle more chocolate crumbs over the top. Place a few chocolate twigs over the top of the dessert, and finally sprinkle with some popping candy.

Notes: Chocolate-coated popping candy can be found at candy stores or specialist cookware and fine food stores.
Siphon guns (also called a whipping siphon), along with the canisters, can be found at chef supply outlets.

Billy's famous ROCKY ROAD

I FIND CLASSIC ROCKY ROAD TO BE OVERLY SWEET, AND I ONLY NEED ONE SMALL PIECE TO SEND ME BUZZING ABOUT ON A SUGAR HIGH. I ALSO THINK THAT SOMETIMES TRADITIONAL RECIPES NEED TO BE REVISED TO BETTER SUIT MODERN DAY PALATES. FOR THIS RECIPE, I USE DARK CHOCOLATE, WHICH HAS A LOWER SUGAR CONTENT THAN MILK CHOCOLATE, THEN BULK IT UP WITH CRISPY RICE BUBBLES. THE TARTNESS OF THE FRESH RASPBERRIES OFFSETS THE SWEETNESS OF THE CHOCOLATE NICELY.

100 g (3½ oz) unsalted butter
250 g (9 oz) dark chocolate (72–75%)
60 g (2 oz/2 cups) Rice Bubbles
180 g (6½ oz/2 cups) marshmallows
1 × 150 g (5 oz) punnet raspberries
70 g (2½ oz/½ cup) pistachio nuts, toasted

1 Grease a 20 cm (8 inch) square baking tin and line the base and sides with baking paper.

2 Melt the butter and chocolate in a heatproof bowl over a saucepan of simmering water over low heat. Do not let the water touch the base of the bowl. Stir occasionally until the chocolate has melted, then remove the pan from the heat and set aside to cool a little.

3 Put the rice bubbles, marshmallows, raspberries and pistachios in a large mixing bowl. Pour in the melted chocolate and stir to combine well. Tip the mixture into the baking tin, spreading it evenly to fill all the corners. Cover the top with a piece of baking paper, place another square baking tin on the top and weigh it down with heavy objects like tins or jars. Transfer to the refrigerator to set for at least 1 hour. Slice into 5 cm (2 inch) pieces.

MAKES
16

THERE IS SOMETHING DELICIOUSLY DECADENT ABOUT CUTTING OPEN A CHOCOLATE FONDANT. I LOVE THE FLOW OF GOOEY DARK CHOCOLATE SAUCE THAT OOZES OUT LIKE MOLTEN LAVA.

You SAUCY THING, you!

CHOCOLATE FONDANT

unsalted butter, for greasing
2 tablespoons cocoa powder
*100 g (3½ oz) dark chocolate
(70%), roughly chopped*
100 g (3½ oz) unsalted butter
2 eggs
2 egg yolks
*50 g (2 oz/¼ cup) caster
(superfine) sugar*
*50 g (2 oz/⅓ cup) plain
(all-purpose) flour*

SWEET SABLE CRUMBS

*50 g (2 oz) chilled unsalted
butter, cut into 1 cm
(½ inch) cubes*
*50 g (2 oz/¼ cup) caster
(superfine) sugar*
*150 g (5 oz/1 cup) plain
(all-purpose) flour*
pinch of salt

2 bananas
55 g (2 oz/¼ cup) sugar
*125 ml (4 fl oz/½ cup) Salted
caramel (page 246)*
*Peanut butter ice cream
(page 262)*

SERVES

4

1 To make the chocolate fondant, use a pastry brush to grease four 125 ml (4 fl oz/½ cup) dariole moulds with butter. It is important to brush the butter upwards along the inside of each mould. Chill the moulds for 10 minutes. Take them out and grease them for a second time, then sprinkle cocoa into one mould, tilting the mould sideways and rotating it so the cocoa gradually coats the inside. Tip the cocoa into the second mould and repeat the process until all moulds are coated. Put the moulds in the refrigerator to set while preparing the fondant.

2 Melt the chocolate and butter in a heatproof bowl over a saucepan of simmering water over low heat. Do not let the water touch the base of the bowl. Stir occasionally until the chocolate has melted, then remove the pan from the heat and set aside to cool.

3 In a separate bowl, put the eggs, egg yolks and sugar and whisk until combined. Pour the chocolate mixture into the bowl and stir well. Gently fold the flour into the mixture. Pour mixture into the moulds, filling each one to about 1 cm (½ inch) below the rim. Refrigerate to set for at least 1 hour, or overnight.

4 Meanwhile, to make the sable crumbs, preheat the oven to 180°C (350°F). Line a baking tray with baking paper. Put all the ingredients in a mixing bowl, then use your fingertips to rub the butter into the flour until the mixture resembles fine breadcrumbs. Spread the crumbs on the prepared baking tray and bake for 15 minutes, or until golden brown. Remove and allow to cool, then put the crumbs in a bowl. Using a hand-held stick blender, pulse a few times to break down the big clumps. Store in a plastic container for later use.

5 Increase the oven to 220°C (430°F). Put the chocolate fondant ramekins on a baking tray and bake for 14–15 minutes, or until the top of the fondant is cooked but is still soft to the touch. Remove from the oven and let them rest for few minutes, then run a knife along the inside of the mould to make sure the fondant is not stuck (but leave them in the moulds for now).

6 Meanwhile, cut off both ends of the bananas, then cut them in half. Then, for each half, halve them again but diagonally. You should now have 8 banana pieces with a flat base. Sprinkle sugar on top of the banana pieces, then burn the sugar with a kitchen blowtorch until caramelised and dark brown.

7 To serve, place a tablespoon of salted caramel on each serving plate, then flip the fondant over onto the plate and remove the mould. Sprinkle a tablespoon of sweet sable crumbs on the side, then top with a quenelle of peanut butter ice cream. Place 2 banana slices next to the ice cream.

Chewy wookie
CHOC CHIP COOKIE

WHY SETTLE ON A SMALL COOKIE, WHEN YOU CAN HAVE A MASSIVE ONE? IF YOU LIKE YOUR COOKIE SOFT AND CHEWY, THEN THIS COOKIE BAKED IN A SKILLET MIGHT BE JUST WHAT YOU'VE BEEN LOOKING FOR. IT'S ALMOST LIKE BAKING A CAKE, BUT THE HEAVY CAST-IRON PAN, WHICH CONDUCTS THE HEAT EFFECTIVELY, GIVES THE COOKIE A NICE CHEWY SHELL. IT'S A GREAT PARTY DESSERT TO SHARE WITH FRIENDS: SIMPLY PLACE THE PAN IN THE MIDDLE OF THE TABLE AND LET EVERYONE CUT OFF A WEDGE, AS SMALL OR LARGE AS THEY WANT. IT IS SERIOUSLY TO DIE FOR (NOT LITERALLY, OF COURSE).

75 g ($2\frac{1}{2}$ oz/$\frac{1}{2}$ cup) plain (all-purpose) flour

pinch of sea salt

$\frac{1}{2}$ teaspoon baking powder

200 g (7 oz) dark chocolate (70%), roughly chopped

100 g ($3\frac{1}{2}$ oz) unsalted butter

3 eggs

110 g ($3\frac{3}{4}$ oz/$\frac{1}{2}$ cup firmly packed) dark brown sugar

110 g ($3\frac{3}{4}$ oz/$\frac{1}{2}$ cup) caster (superfine) sugar

1 teaspoon vanilla extract

85 g (3 oz/$\frac{1}{2}$ cup) dark chocolate chips (60%)

100 g ($3\frac{1}{2}$ oz/1 cup) pecans, toasted

15 g ($\frac{1}{2}$ oz/$\frac{1}{4}$ cup) dried barberries (see note)

1 Preheat the oven to 170°C (340°F). Grease a 25 cm (10 inch) enamel cast-iron skillet pan and set aside. Sift the flour, salt and baking powder into a bowl and set aside.

2 Melt the chocolate and butter in a heatproof bowl over a saucepan of simmering water over low heat. Do not let the water touch the base of the bowl. Stir occasionally until the chocolate has melted, then remove the pan from the heat and set aside to cool.

3 Put the eggs, brown sugar, caster sugar and vanilla in the bowl of an electric mixer and whisk on high speed for about 2 minutes, or until light and creamy. Reduce the speed to medium–low, then pour the melted chocolate and then the flour into the mixture and whisk until just combined. Turn the mixer off, and add the chocolate chips, pecans and barberries. Use a spatula to fold them into the mixture.

4 Pour the mixture into the greased skillet, then bake in the oven for 35–40 minutes. The cookie should be crusty on the edges, and the centre should be just set but still a little gooey inside. Remove from the oven and let it rest in the skillet to finish cooking and cool down completely. Serve the cookie straight from the pan with clotted cream or ice cream.

Note: Barberries are small red berries with a very sharp, sour flavour and are often used in Middle Eastern cooking. Look for them in fine food stores. If unavailable, use dried cranberries, cherries or redcurrants.

Lemon myrtle DELICIOUS

SERVES 4

WHEN IT COMES TO DESSERTS, I LOVE EXPLORING NEW FLAVOURS AND EXPERIMENTING WITH EXCITING INGREDIENTS: AUSTRALIAN NATIVE HERBS FOR INSTANCE. I'VE REVIVED THIS RETRO SELF-SAUCING BEAUTY BY INFUSING IT WITH LEMON MYRTLE LEAVES, WHICH GIVE IT AN ADDED HINT OF LEMONGRASS FLAVOUR. THIS IS A GREAT RECIPE TO HAVE IN YOUR DESSERT REPERTOIRE.

10 lemon myrtle leaves
250 ml ($8\frac{1}{2}$ fl oz/1 cup) full-cream milk
55 g (2 oz) unsalted butter, at room temperature
110 g ($3\frac{3}{4}$ oz/$\frac{1}{2}$ cup) sugar
2 eggs, separated
55 g (2 oz/$\frac{1}{3}$ cup) self-raising flour
finely grated zest and juice of 1 lemon
250 ml ($8\frac{1}{2}$ fl oz/1 cup) thickened (whipping) cream (35% fat)
4 tablespoons icing (confectioners') sugar

1 Preheat the oven to 200°C (400°F). Put the lemon myrtle leaves and milk in a saucepan and heat to boiling point, then remove from the heat and set aside for 10 minutes to let the lemon myrtle leaves infuse the milk. Strain the milk into a jug, discarding the leaves.

2 Beat the butter and sugar using an electric mixer on high speed until pale and creamy. Then turn the speed to low, add the egg yolks and flour and mix until combined. Pour the milk into the mixture and continue to beat until it forms a smooth batter. Add the lemon zest and juice, and mix well.

3 Whisk the egg whites in a clean, dry mixing bowl until soft peaks form. Whisk a third of the egg white into the batter until well combined, then fold the remaining egg white into the batter in two halves, making sure you are very gentle when folding so you don't knock the air out.

4 Pour the mixture into a 20 cm (8 inch) cast-iron pan and bake in the oven for 20–25 minutes until the top is golden brown. Meanwhile, whip the cream and icing sugar until stiff.

5 Serve immediately while still hot, with a dollop of whipped cream, or sprinkle with icing sugar and serve with a big scoop of vanilla ice cream.

Tarts – PASSIONFRUIT MERINGUE; MACADAMIA & SALTED CARAMEL; NO-BAKE KEY LIME; CHILLI CHOCOLATE GANACHE; CHOCOLATE & PEANUT BUTTER;

I LOVE MAKING TARTS FOR AFTERNOON TEA, PICNICS, PARTIES OR SIMPLY WHENEVER I CRAVE FOR SWEET TREATS. THESE ARE A FEW OF MY FAVOURITES BUT, MOST IMPORTANTLY, THEY ARE SIMPLY DELICIOUS AND DIVINE.

SWEET PASTRY
tart cases

125 g (4 oz) chilled unsalted
  butter, cut into cubes

30 g (1 oz) caster (superfine)
  sugar

200 g (7 oz/1⅓ cups) plain
  (all-purpose) flour, plus
  extra for dusting

pinch of salt

4 tablespoons chilled water

MAKES
8*
___
* MAKES
8 TART
CASES

1 Put all the ingredients, except the water, into a food processor and pulse until it resembles breadcrumbs. Then add the water, 1 tablespoon at a time, and keep pulsing until it comes together and forms rough dough. Place the dough on a floured surface and gently knead it a few times until smooth. Flatten the dough into a disc about 2 cm (¾ inch) thick, then wrap in plastic wrap and place in the refrigerator for at least 2 hours, or overnight.

2 Remove the pastry from the refrigerator. Lightly dust the pastry, work surface and rolling pin with flour, then roll out the pastry to a 3 mm (⅛ inch) thickness. Using an 11 cm (4¼ inch) round pastry cutter, cut out 8 rounds from the pastry.

3 Line the individual tart tins with the pastry: use your index fingers and thumbs to gently push the pastry into the corners of the tins. Try not to stretch the pastry too much or it will shrink when baking. Once all the tart tins are lined with pastry, place them on a baking tray and transfer to the freezer to chill for 20 minutes, so the pastry holds its shape when baking.

4 Preheat the oven to 200°C (400°F). Line the tart shells with baking paper, then fill with pastry weights, rice or dried beans. Transfer to the oven and blind bake the tart cases for 20–25 minutes, or until they are golden and crisp. Remove from the oven and let them cool a little before removing the blind baking materials and the tins.

4 tart cases (opposite)

PASSIONFRUIT CURD
75 g (2½ oz/⅓ cup) sugar
125 ml (4 fl oz/½ cup)
    full-cream milk
250 ml (8½ fl oz/1 cup)
    thickened (whipping)
    cream (35% fat)
3 egg yolks, lightly beaten
170 g (6 oz) tinned
    passionfruit pulp

ITALIAN MERINGUE
150 g (5 oz/⅔ cup) caster
    (superfine) sugar
100 ml (3½ fl oz) water
3 egg whites

WHEN I FIRST TASTED
ADRIANO ZUMBO'S
PASSIONFRUIT TART, I WAS
HOOKED. THIS IS A DIVINE
SUMMERY TART WITH THE
EXOTIC FRAGRANCE OF
PASSIONFRUIT. OF COURSE
YOU CAN SUBSTITUTE
THE PASSIONFRUIT CURD
WITH LEMON CURD TOO
(PAGE 228).

1 To make the passionfruit curd, put the sugar, milk and cream in a saucepan and bring to boiling point. Remove the milk mixture from the heat and slowly pour into the bowl with the beaten egg yolks. Whisk constantly to stop the mixture curdling. Add the passionfruit pulp and mix well.

2 Pour the mixture back into the pan over very low heat, and stir constantly with a silicone spatula until the mixture has thickened. Pass the custard through a fine sieve and pour into a jug; discard the passionfruit seeds. Set aside to cool down.

3 Put 4 tart cases on a tray. Fill them to the brim with the passionfruit curd, then refrigerate for 2 hours to set.

4 To make the Italian meringue, place a sugar thermometer in a saucepan, add the sugar and water, and stir over medium heat. Once

the sugar has dissolved, stop stirring and turn the heat up to high and let it boil. Once the temperature of the sugar syrup reaches 110°C (230°F), start whisking the egg whites in the bowl of an electric stand mixer to soft peaks.

5 This step is the crucial part. When the sugar syrup reaches 115°C (240°F), remove the pan from the heat immediately. With the mixer on low speed, slowly pour the hot sugar syrup into the egg whites by dripping it down the side of the mixing bowl, to avoid any catching on the beaters and crystallising. Turn the mixer to medium speed and whisk for a further 10 minutes until the meringue is cool and glossy. Scrape the meringue into a piping bag.

6 Pipe the meringue onto the top of the passionfruit curd until it is completely covered. Use a kitchen blowtorch to lightly scorch the meringue all over.

PASSIONFRUIT MERINGUE TARTS

MAKES
4

MACADAMIA & SALTED CARAMEL TARTS

GO NUTS WITH A TART! FOR THIS RECIPE I'VE CHOSEN MACADAMIAS, AS THEY ARE ONE OF THE MOST DELICIOUS NUTS AROUND. THE CRUNCH OF MACADAMIAS GOES WELL WITH THE SOFT SALTED CARAMEL AND THE THICK CHOCOLATE GANACHE ON TOP.

4 tart cases (page 244)
150 g (5 oz) macadamia nuts, halved

SALTED CARAMEL
115 g (4 oz/½ cup) caster (superfine) sugar
125 ml (4 fl oz/½ cup) water
250 ml (8½ fl oz/1 cup) thickened (whipping) cream (35% fat)
1 teaspoon sea salt flakes
50 g (2 oz) unsalted butter, cut into cubes

CHOCOLATE GLAZE
100 g (3½ oz) dark chocolate (75%), roughly chopped
50 g (2 oz) unsalted butter
125 ml (4 fl oz/½ cup) thickened (whipping) cream (35% fat)

1 To make the salted caramel, put the sugar and water into a saucepan over medium heat and stir until the sugar has dissolved. Then turn the heat up to high and stop stirring; let it boil for about 5 minutes until the sugar starts to caramelise and turn into toffee. Keep an eye on it, as the sugar changes colour rather quickly. Once it reaches a dark golden colour, pour the cream into the hot sugar; be very careful as it will splatter. Keep stirring with a wooden spoon and bring the caramel back to the boil, then add the salt and cook for 3 minutes. Remove the pan from the heat. Whisk the butter, a cube at a time, into the caramel, then pour it into a heatproof jug and set aside to cool.

2 Put 4 tart cases on a tray and fill them sparingly with macadamia nuts in a single layer. Do not overcrowd and save some space for the salted caramel. Pour the salted caramel into the tart cases until almost full, about 3 mm (⅛ inch) from the brim. Transfer to the freezer to set for 30 minutes.

3 To make the chocolate glaze, put the chocolate and butter in a heatproof bowl. Heat the cream in a saucepan until boiling point, then quickly remove from the heat and pour over the chocolate. Let the chocolate soften for a minute, then stir until the chocolate has melted. Set aside to cool.

4 Take the tarts out of the freezer and pour the chocolate glaze over the top, filling each case to the brim. Set at room temperature before serving.

MAKES
4

NO-BAKE KEY LIME TARTS

THIS HAS TO BE ONE OF MY FAVOURITE SOUTHERN AMERICAN DESSERTS. TECHNICALLY, I CAN'T REALLY CALL THIS A KEY LIME TART SINCE WE CAN'T GET KEY LIMES IN AUSTRALIA. BUT NOTHING IS GOING TO STOP ME TAKING A BIG BITE INTO THIS LIMEY TART AND PICTURING MYSELF RELAXING IN THE SUNSHINE IN THE FLORIDA KEYS.

4 tart cases (page 244)
125 ml (4 fl oz/½ cup) lime juice
finely grated zest of 1 lime
395 g (14 oz) tinned sweetened
  condensed milk

1 Put 4 tart cases on a tray. Combine the lime juice, lime zest and condensed milk in a bowl. Pour the mixture into a jug and then pour into the tart cases, filling them to the brim. Place in the refrigerator to set for 2–3 hours.

- 200 g (7 oz) dark chocolate (65%), roughly chopped
- 125 ml (4 fl oz/½ cup) thickened (whipping) cream (35% fat)
- 1 teaspoon cayenne pepper, plus extra for dusting
- 4 tart cases (page 244)
- Chocolate glaze (page 246)

1 To make the filling, put the chocolate in a heatproof bowl. Heat the cream in a saucepan until boiling point, then quickly remove from the heat and pour over the chocolate. Let the chocolate soften for a minute, then stir until the chocolate has melted. Add the cayenne pepper and stir to mix well. Set aside to cool.

2 Put 4 tart cases on a tray and pour the chocolate mixture into the cases until almost full, about 3 mm (⅛ inch) from the brim. Place in the refrigerator to set for 30 minutes.

3 Meanwhile, prepare the chocolate glaze, then take the tarts out of the refrigerator and pour the glaze on top, filling each case to the brim. Set at room temperature, then sprinkle with extra cayenne pepper before serving.

MAKES
4

CHILLI CHOCOLATE GANACHE TARTS

CHILLI AND CHOCOLATE GO HAND IN HAND, BUT YOU DON'T WANT TO OVERDO IT. THE CAYENNE PEPPER ADDED TO THE CHOCOLATE IS JUST ENOUGH TO GIVE YOU A NICE HEAT SENSATION ON THE PALATE; IT ALSO HELPS TO ENHANCE THE RICHNESS OF THE CHOCOLATE.

CHOCOLATE & PEANUT BUTTER TARTS

REESE'S PEANUT BUTTER CUPS ARE MY ULTIMATE WEAKNESS: PEANUT BUTTER, CHOCOLATE GANACHE, BUTTERY TART CASE — ENOUGH SAID.

4 tart cases (page 244)
8 tablespoons peanut butter
1 tablespoon caster (superfine) sugar
100 g (3½ oz) dark chocolate (65%), roughly chopped
3 tablespoons thickened (whipping) cream (35% fat)

1 Put 4 tart cases on a tray. Mix the peanut butter and sugar together in a bowl. Put 2 tablespoons of the peanut butter mixture in each tart case, then use a palette knife to slowly spread it around the case. Smooth with the knife, then place in the refrigerator to set.

2 Put the chocolate in a heatproof bowl. Heat the cream in a saucepan until boiling point, then pour the hot cream over the chocolate. Let the chocolate soften for a minute, then stir until the chocolate has melted.

3 Take the tarts out of the refrigerator and pour in the chocolate, filling each case to the brim. Let them set at room temperature before serving.

MAKES

4

Flourless CHOCOLATE CAKE with morello CHERRIES

60 g (2 oz) almond meal (ground almonds)

60 g (2 oz/½ cup) icing (confectioners') sugar, plus extra for dusting

200 g (7 oz) dark chocolate (70%)

200 g (7 oz) unsalted butter

200 g (7 oz) caster (superfine) sugar, plus 110 g (3¾ oz/½ cup) extra

5 eggs

200 g (7 oz) bottled morello cherries, drained on paper towel

250 ml (8½ fl oz/1 cup) thickened (whipping) cream (35% fat)

2 tablespoons Grand Marnier liqueur

1 × 150 g (5 oz) punnet blueberries

1 × 250 g (9 oz) strawberries

1 Preheat the oven to 180°C (350°F). Grease a 21 cm (8¼ inch) springform cake tin and line the base with baking paper. Put the almond meal and icing sugar in a food processor and process for 30 seconds until it is powdery fine.

2 Melt the chocolate and butter in a large heatproof bowl over a saucepan of barely simmering water over low heat. Do not let the water touch the base of the bowl. Stir occasionally until the chocolate has melted, then remove the bowl from the heat.

3 Add the sugar and stir well. Break the eggs into the mixture, one at a time, stirring after each addition until fully incorporated. Fold in the almond meal mixture until combined, then add the cherries and stir well.

4 Pour the mixture into the tin, then place the tin on a baking tray and bake in the oven for 40–45 minutes. The cake should be still slightly moist in the centre. Remove from the oven and leave to cool completely. Don't worry if the cake starts to sink a little as it cools.

5 Meanwhile, put the cream and extra caster sugar in a mixing bowl and whisk until soft peaks form. Add the liqueur, stirring to mix well.

6 Once the cake is completely cool, remove from the tin and transfer to a serving plate. Spread the whipped cream over the top of the cake, then top with as many strawberries and blueberries as you like. Sift icing sugar over the cake before serving.

THIS GLUTEN-FREE DESSERT IS POSSIBLY ONE OF THE EASIEST
RECIPES TO FOLLOW IN THIS COOKBOOK — AND ONE OF THE
MOST DELICIOUS ONES TOO! BASICALLY THE CAKE IS HALF-
BAKED, WITH A SOFT UNDERCOOKED CENTRE, WHICH WILL
BECOME THICK AND FUDGY ONCE SET IN THE REFRIGERATOR.
YOU CAN SUBSTITUTE THE MORELLO CHERRIES WITH
RASPBERRIES, PITTED FRESH CHERRIES OR SUGAR PLUMS.

PETE'S MUM'S
fail-proof
TREACLE PUDDING

THE FUNNY THING ABOUT THIS TREACLE PUDDING IS THERE'S NO TREACLE IN IT! THIS IS A RECIPE FROM MY PARTNER PETE'S MUM, AND THIS IS WHAT SHE CALLS IT BACK IN ENGLAND. TREACLE OR NO TREACLE, SHE SWEARS THAT IT'S FAIL-PROOF. AND TO MAKE LIFE A LITTLE EASIER, THE PUDDING IS COOKED IN A MICROWAVE INSTEAD OF BY THE TRADITIONAL METHOD OF STEAMING IT. IT'S VERY IMPORTANT TO TURN THE POWER OF THE MICROWAVE DOWN, OR YOU WILL END UP WITH A DRY, CRUMBLY SPONGE — FIT ONLY FOR FEEDING THE BIRDS.

50 g (2 oz) unsalted butter, softened

50 g (2 oz/¼ cup) caster (superfine) sugar

1 egg, lightly beaten

a few drops of vanilla essence (optional)

100 g (3½ oz/⅔ cup) self-raising flour

3 tablespoons skim or full-cream milk

90 g (3 oz/¼ cup) golden syrup, plus extra to serve

30 g (1 oz) macadamia nuts, toasted and roughly chopped

1 Beat the butter and sugar using a hand-held whisk until pale and creamy. Add the egg, vanilla and flour and whisk until smooth. Gradually pour the milk into the mixture, whisking until it forms a smooth batter.

2 Grease a heatproof glass bowl or a 500 ml (17 fl oz/2 cup) porcelain pudding basin. Put the golden syrup in the bowl, then pour the batter over the top. Gently tap the bowl on the kitchen bench to level the surface.

3 Set the microwave power to medium–low (30% or 50%, according to the manufacturer's instructions), and cook the pudding for 7 minutes, or until the centre of the pudding is still slightly moist. Leave to stand for 5 minutes before turning the pudding out onto a serving plate. Drizzle another spoonful of golden syrup over the top, then sprinkle with the macadamias. Serve with custard or vanilla ice cream.

SERVES

4

Ondeh ondeh

{COCONUT GLUTINOUS RICE BALLS}

ONDEH-ONDEH IS MY ALL-TIME FAVOURITE SNACK; THESE LITTLE COCONUT-COATED PANDAN-FLAVOURED RICE BALLS ARE ADDICTIVELY CHEWY AND STRETCHY, BUT THE BEST PART IS DEFINITELY THE GULA MELAKA (PALM SUGAR) FILLING INSIDE, WHICH LITERALLY EXPLODES IN YOUR MOUTH WITH A SQUELCH OF LIQUID PALM SUGAR SYRUP. YOU SIMPLY CAN'T STOP AT ONE.

10 pandan (screw pine)
leaves (or 1 teaspoon
pandan essence) (see note
page 93)
150 ml (5 fl oz) water
100 g (3½ oz) gula melaka
(dark palm sugar), grated
(see note)

150 g (5 oz) glutinous
rice flour
1 tablespoon tapioca starch
2 tablespoons icing
(confectioners') sugar
130 g (4½ oz/1½ cups)
desiccated coconut
pinch of salt

1 Put the pandan leaves and water in a blender and blend into a juice. Strain the pandan juice through a fine sieve into a jug, discarding the solids.

2 Take a pinch of grated gula melaka and roll it into a ball the size of a 5-cent coin. Repeat with the remaining sugar. Set aside ready to be used.

3 In a large bowl, combine the glutinous rice flour, tapioca starch, icing sugar and strained pandan juice. Using your hands, knead the mixture into a wet dough — it shouldn't be sticky.

4 Bring a pot of water to a rolling boil. Pinch a small piece of the dough (about 20 g/¾ oz) and drop it into the boiling water. Let it cook until it floats to the surface, then scoop it out. Wearing a glove, knead the cooked dough back into the main dough until it forms a smooth and sticky dough. Add a little more flour if the dough is too wet. Set aside for 15 minutes.

5 Meanwhile, mix the desiccated coconut with a pinch of salt. Place the coconut in a steamer lined with baking paper and steam for 5 minutes over a saucepan of simmering water. Spread on a tray to cool completely.

6 Bring the same pot of water to the boil again and have the tray of desiccated coconut ready, as you will have to do a few things at once at this point. Take a small piece of the pandan dough (about 15 g/½ oz) and roll it into a ball, then flatten slightly in your palm. Place a gula melaka ball in the centre, fold the dough over, seal the edges and then roll it back into a ball. Working in batches of 10–15, quickly drop the balls into the boiling water and let them cook while you make more balls with the rest of the dough.

7 Keep an eye on the balls in the pot: once they are cooked, they will float to the surface. Scoop them out with a slotted spoon, shake off the excess water and drop them in the desiccated coconut. Roll them around until they are nicely coated. Let them cool down before transferring to a serving plate.

Note: Gula melaka, or dark palm sugar, is commonly used in Malaysian and Indonesian cooking. Sold in Asian grocers, gula melaka usually comes in a log shape; don't get it mixed up with the light palm sugar, which is usually sold as small discs. Please be mindful to buy sustainable gula melaka, and stop the unethical practice of forest logging that has destroyed much of the orang-utan's habitat in Malaysia and Indonesia.

MAKES
20
TO
30

Vegemite CHEESECAKE

I CAN SEE SOME OF YOU SCREWING UP YOUR FACES AT THE MERE TITLE OF THIS RECIPE. ALL I CAN SAY IS 'DON'T JUDGE IT UNTIL YOU'VE TRIED IT'. AS WE KNOW, SALT BRINGS OUT THE SWEETNESS IN FOOD, AND THIS WORKS THE SAME WAY: THE SALTY VEGEMITE ENHANCES THE SWEETNESS OF THE CHEESECAKE. I ALSO FIND THE YEAST IN THE VEGEMITE HELPS THE CAKE TO RISE BETTER WHEN BAKING, WHICH YIELDS AN AIRIER TEXTURE. ARE YOU CONVINCED YET?

CRUST

250 g (9 oz) plain sweet biscuits

150 g (5 oz) unsalted butter, melted

2 tablespoons caster (superfine) sugar

CHEESECAKE

500 g (1 lb 2 oz) cream cheese, softened

220 g ($7\frac{3}{4}$ oz/1 cup) sugar

3 large eggs

250 ml ($8\frac{1}{2}$ fl oz/1 cup) thickened (whipping) cream (35% fat)

1 tablespoon lemon juice

2 tablespoons Vegemite yeast extract

VEGEMITE CHOCOLATE GANACHE

250 g (9 oz) dark chocolate (70%), roughly chopped

150 ml (5 fl oz) thickened (whipping) cream (35% fat)

1 tablespoon Vegemite yeast extract

SERVES 10 TO 12

1 Preheat the oven to 180°C (350°F). Line the base of a 24 cm ($9\frac{1}{2}$ inch) springform cake tin with baking paper.

2 Mix together the ingredients for the crust, then tip the mixture into the prepared tin and gently press the crumbs evenly over the base and about 5 cm (2 inches) up the side. Place in the refrigerator to set.

3 To make the cheesecake, beat the cream cheese and sugar using an electric mixer until smooth. Add the eggs, one at a time, making sure each egg is fully incorporated before adding the next. Add the cream, lemon juice and Vegemite, and beat until smooth and creamy.

4 Pour the mixture into the prepared crust, tap the tin gently on the bench top to get rid of any air bubbles and level the surface. Wrap the bottom and side of the tin in foil, then place it in a 4 cm ($1\frac{1}{2}$ inch) deep baking dish. Pour boiling water into the baking dish until the water reaches halfway up the side of the cake tin. Make sure there are no tears or holes in the foil; if so, the water may seep into the tin and you'll end up with a soggy crust base.

5 Bake the cheesecake in the oven for 1 hour. It should be just set but still wobbly in the centre. Turn the oven off, and let it cool in the oven for at least an hour. This will allow the cake to finish cooking and prevent cracking on top. Take it out and let it finish cooling on the bench top if it's still warm. Cover with plastic wrap and refrigerate overnight to set.

6 To make the Vegemite chocolate ganache, put the chocolate in a heatproof bowl. Heat the cream in a saucepan until boiling point, then quickly remove from the heat and pour over the chocolate. Let the chocolate soften for a minute, then stir until the chocolate has melted. Add the Vegemite and stir to mix well. Pour the chocolate ganache over the cheesecake, tilting the cheesecake in a circular motion to spread the ganache evenly. Cut into small slices and serve.

Ice cream — COCONUT; AVOCADO; PEANUT BUTTER; MATCHA; GINGERBREAD

HERE ARE FIVE GREAT ICE CREAM FLAVOURS THAT I LOVE TO MAKE, EITHER ON THEIR OWN OR AS A COMPONENT OF A DESSERT. ENJOY!

Coconut
ICE CREAM

THIS IS ONE OF THE SIMPLEST ICE CREAM RECIPES. COCONUT ICE CREAM IS RICH AND CREAMY, AND IS BEST SERVED WITH SOUR OR CITRUSY FRUIT LIKE CARAMELISED PINEAPPLE OR LEMON.

250 ml (8½ fl oz/1 cup) full-cream milk

115 g (4 oz/½ cup) caster (superfine) sugar

6 egg yolks, lightly whisked

250 ml (8½ fl oz/1 cup) thickened (whipping) cream (35% fat)

270 ml (9 fl oz) tinned coconut cream

1 Heat the milk and sugar in a saucepan until simmering, stirring occasionally until the sugar has dissolved. Remove the pan from the heat and slowly pour the hot milk in a steady stream into the egg yolks, whisking continuously so the eggs don't curdle. Once combined, pour the mixture back into the saucepan and keep stirring over low heat until thickened. The mixture should be thick enough to coat the back of a spatula when it is ready. Remove from the heat and set aside to cool for 10 minutes.

2 Pour the cream and coconut cream into the mixture, stirring until combined. Cover and refrigerate for at least 2 hours, or overnight.

3 Churn the mixture in an ice-cream maker according to the manufacturer's directions. It will take 15–20 minutes for the ice cream to set. Serve immediately, or transfer to a container and store in the freezer for a firmer texture.

Avocado
ICE CREAM

MY FIRST TASTE OF AVOCADO IN A DESSERT WAS DURING MY TRIP TO VIETNAM IN 2009. THE AVOCADO WAS BLITZED WITH CONDENSED MILK AND ICE INTO A SMOOTHIE. IT WAS THICK AND SMOOTH, LIKE A MEAL IN A CUP! THIS AVOCADO ICE CREAM IS LOVELY AND SWEET BUT I'VE ADDED A GOOD SPLASH OF LIME JUICE TO GIVE IT A NICE ZING; THE LIME ALSO PREVENTS THE LOVELY GREEN AVOCADO FROM OXIDIZING AND TURNING BROWN.

250 ml (8½ fl oz/1 cup) thickened (whipping) cream (35% fat)

3 ripe avocados, halved and stones removed

250 ml (8½ fl oz/1 cup) full-cream milk

170 g (6 oz/¾ cup) caster (superfine) sugar

1 tablespoon freshly squeezed lime juice

pinch of salt

1 Whip the cream in a large bowl until soft peaks form, then set aside.

2 Scrape the avocado flesh into a food processor, add the milk, sugar, lime juice and salt, and process to a smooth purée. Pour the mixture into the whipped cream. Using a spatula, gently fold the mixture into the cream until just combined. Cover and refrigerate for 4–6 hours, or overnight.

3 Churn the mixture in an ice-cream maker according to the manufacturer's directions. It will take 15–20 minutes for the ice cream to set. Serve immediately, or transfer to a container and store in the freezer for a firmer texture.

SERVES
6-8

375 ml (13 fl oz/1½ cups) full-cream milk

115 g (4 oz/½ cup) caster (superfine) sugar

2 tablespoons honey

3 egg yolks, lightly whisked

375 ml (13 fl oz/1½ cups) thickened (whipping) cream (35% fat)

250 g (9 oz/1 cup) smooth peanut butter

1 Heat the milk, sugar and honey in a saucepan until simmering, stirring occasionally until the sugar has dissolved. Remove the pan from the heat and slowly pour the hot milk mixture in a steady stream into the egg yolks, whisking continuously so the eggs don't curdle. Once combined, pour the mixture back into the saucepan and keep stirring over low heat until thickened. The mixture should be thick enough to coat the back of a spatula when it is ready. Remove from the heat and set aside to cool for 10 minutes.

2 Add the cream and peanut butter to the mixture, stirring until combined. Strain the mixture through a fine sieve to get rid of any lumps. Cover and refrigerate for at least 2 hours, or overnight.

3 Churn the mixture in an ice-cream maker according to the manufacturer's directions. It will take 15–20 minutes for the ice cream to set. Serve immediately, or transfer to a container and store in the freezer for a firmer texture.

SERVES
6-8

AFTER CHOCOLATE, PEANUT BUTTER IS MY SECOND LOVE. THIS ICE CREAM GOES WELL WITH MANY DESSERTS; TRY IT WITH CHEWY WOOKIE CHOC-CHIP COOKIE (PAGE 238) OR YOU SAUCY THING, YOU! (PAGE 236).

Peanut butter
ICE CREAM

Matcha
ICE CREAM

I FELL IN LOVE WITH MATCHA ICE CREAM WHEN I WENT TO JAPAN. IT IS NOT AS RICH AS OTHER ICE CREAMS, BUT THE SUBTLE GREEN TEA FLAVOUR IS REFRESHING — PERFECT FOR SUMMER DAYS. GREEN TEA IS CHOCK FULL OF ANTIOXIDANTS, SO SURELY THIS IS GOOD FOR YOU ... ISN'T IT?

375 ml (13 fl oz/1½ cups) thickened (whipping) cream (35% fat)

375 ml (13 fl oz/1½ cups) full-cream milk

115 g (4 oz/½ cup) caster (superfine) sugar

2 tablespoons matcha powder (Japanese green tea)

1 Whip the cream in a large bowl until soft peaks form, then set aside.

2 Put the milk, sugar and matcha powder into a food processor and process until well combined and the sugar has dissolved. Strain the mixture through a fine sieve into the whipped cream. Fold the cream gently into the mixture, then cover and refrigerate for at least 2 hours, or overnight.

3 Churn the mixture in an ice-cream maker according to the manufacturer's directions. It will take 15–20 minutes for the ice cream to set. Serve immediately, or transfer to a container and store in the freezer for a firmer texture.

SERVES
6-8

Gingerbread
ICE CREAM

EVERY TIME I MAKE THIS ICE CREAM, MY HOUSE FILLS WITH THE INCREDIBLE AROMAS OF SPICES. SERVE THIS ICE CREAM WITH POACHED PEARS, OR OMIT THE ICE CREAM PART AND JUST MAKE THE GINGERBREAD COOKIES ON THEIR OWN. THE RECIPE MAKES 20–24 GINGERBREAD MEN.

250 ml (8½ fl oz/1 cup) full-cream milk
160 g (5½ oz/¾ cup firmly packed) light brown sugar
5 egg yolks, lightly whisked
1 tablespoon ground ginger
½ teaspoon ground cinnamon
½ teaspoon ground nutmeg
375 ml (13 fl oz/1½ cups) thickened (whipping) cream (35% fat)
150 g (5 oz/1 cup) crumbled gingerbread biscuit (recipe below)

GINGERBREAD BISCUIT

100 g (3½ oz) unsalted butter, softened
100 g (3½ oz) dark brown sugar
80 g (3 oz) golden syrup
1 egg
1 egg yolk
300 g (10½ oz/2 cups) plain (all-purpose) flour
pinch of salt
½ teaspoon bicarbonate of soda (baking soda)
2½ teaspoons ground ginger
½ teaspoon ground cinnamon
½ teaspoon ground nutmeg

1 To make the gingerbread biscuit, beat the butter, brown sugar and golden syrup using an electric mixer on high speed until light and creamy. Turn the speed to medium/low, add the egg and egg yolk and mix until well combined.

2 Sift the remaining dry ingredients into a bowl. Turn the speed on the electric mixer to low and, working in 3 batches, add the dry ingredients, mixing until combined. Gather the dough together and flatten into a disc. Cover with plastic wrap and refrigerate for 1 hour, or until it is firm enough to be rolled out.

3 Preheat the oven to 165°C (330°F). Line a baking tray with baking paper. Transfer the dough to a lightly floured surface and roll out to a 3 mm (⅛ inch) thickness. Place the dough on the tray and bake for 20 minutes, or until lightly golden. Transfer the biscuits to a wire rack.

4 To make the ice cream, heat the milk and brown sugar in a saucepan until simmering, stirring occasionally until the sugar has dissolved. Remove the pan from the heat and slowly pour the hot milk in a steady stream into the egg yolks, whisking continuously so the eggs don't curdle. Add the ground ginger, cinnamon and nutmeg, pour the mixture back into the saucepan and keep stirring over low heat until thickened. The mixture should be thick enough to coat the back of a spatula when it is ready. Remove from the heat and set aside to cool for 10 minutes. Pour the cream into the mixture, stirring until combined. Cover and refrigerate for at least 2 hours, or overnight.

6 Churn the mixture in an ice-cream maker according to the manufacturer's directions. It will take 1 hour for the ice cream to set. Stir the gingerbread crumbs into the ice cream, transfer into an ice-cream container and sprinkle more crumbs over the top. Cover and refrigerate to set before serving.

Chocolate & SALTED CARAMEL pots de crème

250 ml (8½ fl oz/1 cup) Salted
caramel (page 246)
250 g (9 oz) dark chocolate
(65%), roughly chopped
250 ml (8½ fl oz/1 cup)
full-cream milk

250 ml (8½ fl oz/1 cup)
thickened (whipping)
cream (35% fat), plus
125 ml (4 fl oz/½ cup)
extra for serving
75 g (2½ oz/⅓ cup) caster
(superfine) sugar

120 g (4 oz) egg yolks (about 6)
2 tablespoons icing
(confectioners') sugar
strawberries, for garnish
(optional)

1 Prepare the salted caramel. Place 6–8 ramekins or small cups on a tray.

2 Put the chocolate in the bowl of a food processor. Heat the milk, cream and caster sugar in a saucepan over medium heat, stirring until the sugar has dissolved and the milk starts to boil.

3 Whisk the egg yolks in a bowl. Slowly pour the hot milk mixture into the egg yolk, whisking continuously to stop the yolks from curdling. Pour the mixture back into the saucepan and stir over low heat for about 5 minutes, or until it is thick enough to coat the back of a spatula.

4 Pour the hot mixture over the chocolate in the processor, cover with a kitchen towel to avoid spillage, then blend until combined and all the chocolate has melted.

5 Put 2 tablespoons of salted caramel into each ramekin, then divide the chocolate mixture equally among the ramekins. Transfer to the refrigerator to set for at least 2 hours.

6 Whip the extra cream and icing sugar in a mixing bowl until soft peaks form. When ready to serve, add a dollop of whipped cream on top of the pots de crème and garnish with strawberries, if desired.

MY TECHNIQUE FOR MAKING THESE POTS OF GOODNESS IS TO BLEND THE INGREDIENTS IN A FOOD PROCESSOR. HOWEVER, YOU CAN MAKE THESE POTS DE CRÈME THE TRADITIONAL WAY BY USING A DOUBLE BOILER — ALTHOUGH THEY WON'T BE AS LIGHT IN TEXTURE.

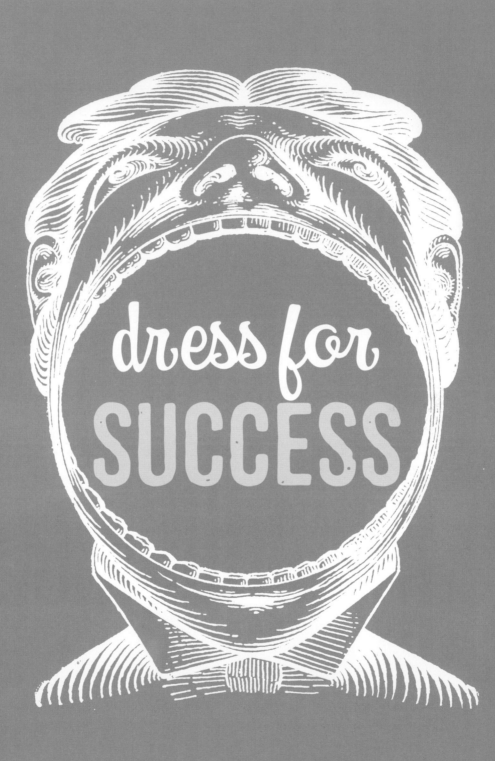

dress for SUCCESS

Nam jim dressing ✦ WASABI
MAYONNAISE ✦ Chimichurri ✦ REMPAH
SPICE PASTE ✦ XO sauce ✦ PICKLED GREEN
CHILLIES ✦ Romesco sauce ✦ CHILLI ONION
JAM ✦ Basil pesto

NAM JIM DRESSING

NAM JIM DRESSING IS ALL ABOUT THE BALANCE OF HOT, SOUR, SALTY AND SWEET; THESE FOUR FLAVOURS SHOULD COMPLEMENT EACH OTHER WITHOUT ONE OVERPOWERING THE OTHER. THERE IS AN OLD WIVES' TALE THAT SAYS THAT IF A GIRL CAN MAKE A GOOD NAM JIM DRESSING, THEN SHE WILL MAKE A VERY GOOD WIFE. I'M NOT SURE IF MY NAM JIM DRESSING MEETS THOSE STANDARDS, BUT IT SURE IS A DAMN GOOD ONE!

3 bird's eye chillies, finely chopped (see note)
2 small French shallots, finely chopped
2 garlic cloves, finely chopped
1 tablespoon thinly sliced coriander (cilantro) roots
2 tablespoons grated palm sugar (jaggery)
2 tablespoons fish sauce
juice of ½ lime

1 Using a mortar and pestle, gently pound the chillies, shallots, garlic and coriander roots to bruise them, without turning them into a paste. Scrape the mixture into a mixing bowl.

2 Add the palm sugar, fish sauce and lime juice, and stir well until the sugar has dissolved. Taste the dressing and adjust accordingly — it should have a good balance of the key elements of hot, sour, salty and sweet. Store the dressing in the refrigerator for up to 3 days, but it's best to make this fresh when needed.

Note: If you want a less spicy dressing, substitute the bird's eye chillies with 1 large red chilli, seeded.

WASABI MAYONNAISE

THIS IS A QUICK AND EASY MAYONNAISE TO MAKE. IF YOU DON'T HAVE A FOOD PROCESSOR, YOU WILL NEED TO USE A HAND WHISK AND LOTS OF ELBOW GREASE. BE PATIENT, DRIZZLE THE OIL SLOWLY INTO THE YOLKS AS YOU WHISK CONTINUOUSLY AND EVENTUALLY IT WILL EMULSIFY AND COME TOGETHER NICELY. IT IS A GREAT MAYONNAISE TO GO WITH PRAWNS (PAGE 36), LOBSTER (PAGE 179) OR DEEP-FRIED SNACKS (PAGE 19).

1 tablespoon wasabi paste
2 egg yolks
1 teaspoon white vinegar
salt and pepper
375 ml (13 fl oz/1½ cups) grapeseed oil
squeeze of lemon juice
pinch of cayenne pepper

1 Place the wasabi paste, egg yolks, vinegar and a pinch of salt in a food processor, and process until combined. With the food processor still running, add the oil in a thin, steady stream — the mixture will start to emulsify and turn into mayonnaise.

2 Scrape the thick mayonnaise into a bowl and season to taste with salt, pepper and lemon juice. Sprinkle with cayenne pepper before serving. Store in the refrigerator for up to 1 week.

Note: Alternatively, you can simply mix 60 g (2 oz) Japanese mayonnaise with the wasabi paste and sprinkle with cayenne pepper.

DRESSINGS ARE THE FOUNDATION OF MANY DELICIOUS CUISINES. WHETHER IT'S MARINADES, CONDIMENTS OR SAUCES, EVERYONE SHOULD HAVE A FEW BASIC RECIPES IN THEIR COOKING REPERTOIRE. THIS CHAPTER SHOWCASES A FEW OF MY FAVOURITES.

CHIMICHURRI

CHIMICHURRI IS AN ARGENTINIAN GREEN SAUCE MADE FROM PARSLEY AND CORIANDER, AND COMMONLY USED FOR GRILLED MEATS AS A MARINADE OR DRESSING — AND I LOVE IT! THIS IS MY VERSION THAT I USE ON ALMOST ANYTHING THAT I CAN LAY MY HANDS ON — TRY IT INSTEAD OF BASIL PESTO ON A PIZZA. IT'S BEST TO MAKE IT JUST BEFORE YOU NEED IT, AND USE IMMEDIATELY BEFORE IT LOSES ITS VIVID GREEN COLOUR.

15 g ($\frac{1}{2}$ oz/1 cup firmly packed)
    flat-leaf (Italian) parsley,
    leaves only
5 g ($\frac{1}{8}$ oz/$\frac{1}{4}$ cup) coriander (cilantro)
    leaves
2 garlic cloves
1 large red chilli
125 ml (4 fl oz/$\frac{1}{2}$ cup) olive oil
3 tablespoons red wine vinegar
salt and pepper, to taste

1 Put the parsley, coriander, garlic, chilli and 2 tablespoons of the olive oil in a food processor or blender, and process into a paste.

2 Scrape the mixture into a bowl, add the vinegar and remaining olive oil and stir well. Season with salt and pepper, to taste. Use immediately.

Note: Leftover sauce can be stored in an airtight jar, but you need to cover the top of the sauce with a good layer of olive oil to stop oxidation. Chimichurri will keep in the refrigerator for up to 1 week.

MAKES
**250
GRAMS**
(9 OZ/1 CUP)

REMPAH SPICE PASTE

MOST MALAYSIAN COOKING, ESPECIALLY NYONYA COOKING, USUALLY STARTS WITH A GOOD CHILLI PASTE AS THE BASE FLAVOUR OF A DISH. THIS SPICY REMPAH PASTE IS VERY VERSATILE AND WILL WORK ACROSS MANY MALAYSIAN DISHES INCLUDING CURRY LAKSA (PAGE 208) AND NYONYA SPICY TAMARIND SNAPPER (PAGE 172).

20 g ($\frac{3}{4}$ oz) belachan (dried shrimp
    paste) (see notes)
10 g ($\frac{1}{2}$ oz) dried red chillies (use less
    or seeded chillies if you don't like
    it too hot), soaked in hot water for
    30 minutes, then drained
5 large fresh red chillies, seeded
10 g ($\frac{1}{2}$ oz) candlenuts, roasted
    (see notes)
5 garlic cloves, peeled
100 g ($3\frac{1}{2}$ oz) French shallots
    (about 10–12), peeled
15 g ($\frac{1}{2}$ oz) fresh turmeric, peeled
    (or 1 tablespoon ground turmeric)
5 g ($\frac{1}{8}$ oz) galangal, peeled
2 lemongrass stalks, white part only

1 Heat a frying pan over medium heat. Wrap the belachan in foil, then put it in the pan and toast the whole thing for 2 minutes on both sides. Remove and let it cool before unwrapping it.

2 Put all the ingredients, including the belachan, into a food processor and process into a fine paste. Use immediately or store in an airtight container in the refrigerator or freezer.

Notes: Belachan, or belacan, is a dried shrimp paste that has quite an offensive pungent aroma when it is cooking, so make sure the kitchen is well ventilated before toasting it.

Candlenuts give the dish a nutty flavour and creamy texture. You can find them at Asian grocers, or substitute cashew or macadamia nuts if unavailable.

MAKES
**300
ML**
(10 FL OZ)

XO SAUCE

INVENTED IN HONG KONG IN THE 80S, XO SAUCE IS A HIGHLY ADDICTIVE CHILLI SAUCE
MADE USING EXPENSIVE INGREDIENTS LIKE SCALLOPS AND HAM. THIS HIGH-QUALITY
PRODUCT WAS CONSIDERED AS PRESTIGIOUS AS THE FRENCH XO COGNAC, AND HENCE
THE NAME. XO SAUCE GOES WELL WITH TOFU, FISH, MEATS AND VEGETABLES, AND IS ALSO A
NICE CONDIMENT TO SERVE WITH NOODLES.

*50 g (2 oz/½ cup)
dried scallops*

*50 g (3 oz/¼ cup)
dried shrimp*

*10 g (½ oz) dried red
chillies (about 20),
seeded then soaked
in hot water for
30 minutes until
softened, then
drained*

*2 large fresh red
chillies, seeded*

*500 ml (17 fl oz/2
cups) vegetable oil,
plus extra*

*1 garlic bulb, cloves
finely chopped*

*50 g (2 oz) French
shallots, finely
diced*

*100 g (3½ oz) pancetta
or prosciutto,
finely shredded*

salt, to taste

MAKES
300
ML
(10 FL OZ)

1 Put the dried scallops and shrimp in a
bowl and add enough water to cover by
about 2 cm (¾ inch). Cover with plastic wrap
and place in the refrigerator to soak until
they are rehydrated and plump, preferably
overnight. Drain and set aside on paper
towel. Put the scallops and shrimp in a food
processor and pulse until roughly chopped;
they should still have a bit of texture.
Transfer to a bowl and set aside.

2 Put the dried and fresh chillies in the
food processor and pulse until roughly
chopped; you should be still able to see
largish specks of chilli. Transfer to a bowl
and set aside.

3 Heat half the vegetable oil in a wok or
large saucepan over medium–high heat,
add the scallops and shrimp and fry for
2 minutes, or until crisp. Add the chillies
and fry for another 2 minutes.

4 Add the remaining oil, the garlic,
shallots and pancetta, turn the heat
down to medium–low, and keep frying for
another 20 minutes or so, stirring
occasionally. The mixture now should be
dark brown with a layer of red chilli oil on
top. Season with salt, to taste.

5 Turn the heat off and leave the sauce
in the wok to cool to room temperature.
Pour the XO sauce into a sterilised jar and
cover with a layer of oil to keep its freshness.
The XO sauce keeps well in the refrigerator
for up to 3 months.

PICKLED GREEN CHILLIES

AT ANY KOPITIAM (COFFEE HOUSE) IN MALAYSIA, INSTEAD OF THE USUAL PAIR OF SALT AND PEPPER SHAKERS, IT IS QUITE COMMON INSTEAD TO FIND A BOTTLE OF CHILLI SAUCE AND A JAR OF PICKLED GREEN CHILLIES ON THE TABLE. THESE PICKLED CHILLIES ARE ACTUALLY NOT HOT AT ALL, BUT HAVE A MORE SOUR AND SWEET FLAVOUR FROM THE PICKLING IN VINEGAR AND SUGAR.

5 large green chillies
125 ml (4 fl oz/½ cup) white vinegar
125 ml (4 fl oz/½ cup) water
2 tablespoons sugar
1 teaspoon salt

1 Cut the green chillies diagonally into thin strips, then place in an airtight glass jar.

2 Add the vinegar, water, sugar and salt, put the lid on and shake the jar vigorously until the sugar and salt have dissolved. Place in the refrigerator to pickle for at least 3 days. The pickled chillies keep well in the refrigerator for up to 3 months — if they don't get eaten before then!

ROMESCO SAUCE

THIS IS MY GO-TO SAUCE FOR ANYTHING SPANISH. I LOVE THE SMOKINESS OF THE GRILLED CAPSICUM, THE NUTTY FLAVOUR OF ALMONDS AND THE HINT OF SPICY HEAT FROM THE CAYENNE PEPPER. ROMESCO SAUCE GOES WELL WITH FISH AND ROASTED POTATOES, AND SOMETIMES I EVEN USE IT ON PIZZA AND PASTA.

1 red capsicum (pepper)
2 garlic cloves, roughly chopped
400 g (14 oz) tinned chopped tomatoes
2½ tablespoons red wine vinegar
2 slices bread, toasted
80 g (3 oz/½ cup) blanched almonds, toasted
3 tablespoons olive oil
1 teaspoon smoked paprika
1 teaspoon cayenne pepper
1 teaspoon salt

1 Place the capsicum on top of a gas stove over a naked flame, turning frequently using kitchen tongs, and let it roast until the skin blackens and blisters on all sides. If you don't have a gas stove, you can roast the capsicum on the barbecue or in the oven under a hot grill (broiler).

2 Put the charred capsicum in a zip-lock bag and let it steam for 10 minutes until softened. Rub the capsicum against the plastic bag to peel the skin off. Remove from the bag and rinse under water, then dry and cut into big chunks. Put the capsicum, garlic, tomatoes, vinegar, bread and almonds in a food processor and process until smooth.

3 Heat the olive oil in a frying pan over medium heat and sauté the capsicum mixture until thickened. Season with smoked paprika, cayenne pepper and salt. Turn off the heat and let it cool in the pan, then pour into an airtight container and store in the refrigerator for up to 1 month.

CHILLI ONION JAM

THIS CHILLI ONION JAM KEEPS WELL IN THE REFRIGERATOR IN AN AIRTIGHT CONTAINER AND IT GOES WELL WITH ALMOST EVERYTHING, SO COOK UP A BIG BATCH OF IT. I LOVE A GOOD SAUSAGE SIZZLE, AND THERE'S NOTHING BETTER THAN A SAUSAGE ON A SLICE OF WHITE BREAD SMOTHERED WITH A BIG DOLLOP OF THIS SWEET CHILLI ONION JAM.

0 tablespoons olive oil
6 onions, thinly sliced
2 large red chillies, seeded and
*   sliced on the diagonal*
3 tablespoons white vinegar
3 tablespoons water
2 tablespoons sugar
1 teaspoon salt
3 tablespoons smoked barbecue
*   sauce*
pinch of cayenne pepper

1 Heat the olive oil in a saucepan over low–medium heat. Add the onions and chillies and cook for about 45–60 minutes, or until the onion softens and turns golden brown. Stir occasionally to make sure the mixture doesn't catch on the base of the saucepan and burn.

2 Add the vinegar, water, sugar and salt, and simmer until the mixture thickens again. Add the barbecue sauce and cayenne pepper, stir for another 10 minutes, then turn off the heat and let it cool completely. Store in a jar in the refrigerator for up to 1 month.

MAKES **180** GRAMS
(6½ OZ/1 CUP)

BASIL PESTO

FRESH BASIL HAS ONE OF THE BEST AROMAS IN THE WORLD! JUST A SMALL DOLLOP OF THIS ITALIAN DRESSING WILL ELEVATE THE FLAVOURS OF A DISH IMMENSELY. IT KEEPS WELL IN THE FRIDGE BUT MAKE SURE TO POUR A LITTLE OLIVE OIL OVER THE TOP TO SEAL THE PESTO FROM THE AIR, TO PREVENT OXIDATION. THIS PESTO IS GREAT WITH PASTA, BUT I OFTEN USE IT WITH HOT BREAKFASTS SUCH AS THE BAKED EGGS WITH CHORIZO (PAGE 97) OR EGGY BREKKY HEART, MY VERSION OF A BREKKY STACK (PAGE 89).

30 g (1 oz/2 cups firmly packed)
*   basil leaves*
40 g (1½ oz/¼ cup) pine nuts, toasted
2 garlic cloves, peeled
50 g (2 oz/½ cup) freshly grated
*   parmesan*
125 ml (4 fl oz/½ cup) olive oil,
*   plus extra*

1 Put all the ingredients into a food processor and blitz to a fine paste. Transfer the pesto into a jar and top it with about 1 cm (½ inch) of olive oil, to stop the pesto from oxidising.

MAKES **250** GRAMS
(9 OZ/1 CUP)

IN MY KITCHEN

1. Mirin
2. Chilli bean sauce
3. Soy sauce
4. Marmite
5. Shaoxing rice wine
6. Preserved beancurd
7. Cooking caramel
8. Fish sauce
9. Worcestershire sauce
10. Dried shrimp
11. Japanese mayonnaise

IN MY KITCHEN

Salmon roe

Cornichons

Lap cheong

Gula melaka

Salted black beans

Light palm sugar

Tamarind peel

Lemon myrtle

Salted radish

Tobiko roe

French shallots

Yellow rock sugar

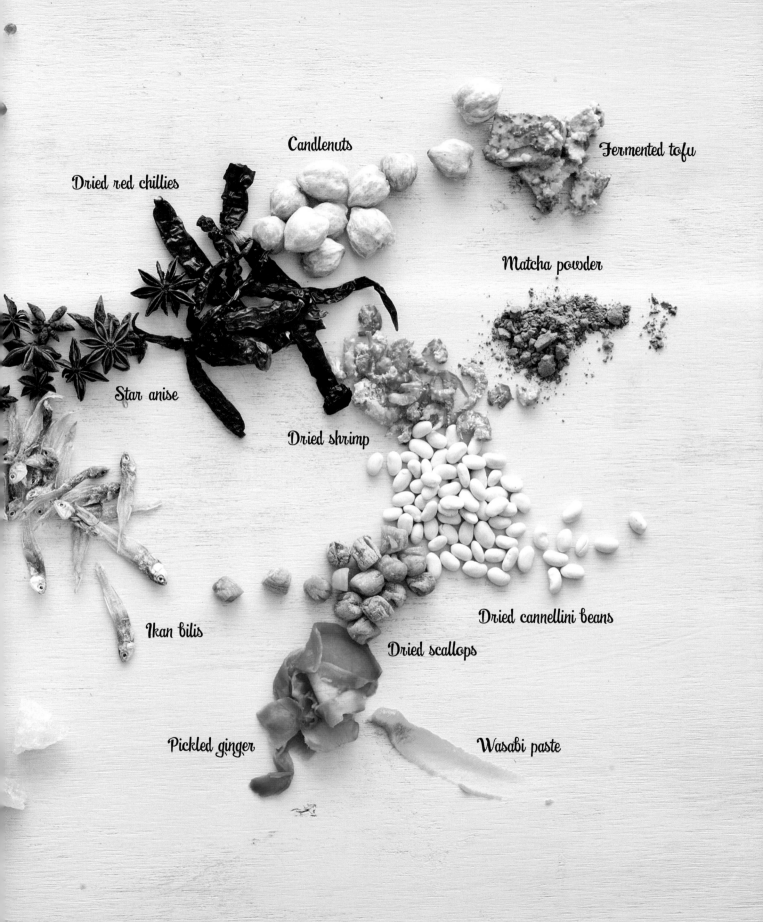

Candlenuts

Fermented tofu

Dried red chillies

Matcha powder

Star anise

Dried shrimp

Dried cannellini beans

Ikan bilis

Dried scallops

Pickled ginger

Wasabi paste

INDEX

Acknowledgements

This cookbook would not have been possible without the following people, to who I extend a big thank you.

To Mum and Dad, for giving me the opportunity to start a new life in Australia and supporting me with the path in life that I've chosen.

To my brothers and sisters — Steven, Vivian, Phooi Leng, Jenny and Chee Ming for accepting who I am and always being there for me whenever I need advice.

Thanks Pete for your unconditional love and always being there for me when I was going through tough times. And thank you for believing in me all this time to let me chase after my dream.

A big shout out to the people at Hardie Grant Books who made this book possible. Paul McNally for giving me this great opportunity, especially for letting me run the entire book from writing, cooking and testing, to photographing and styling; working with you on this cookbook has been a blast. To Heather Menzies for your art direction and turning my imagination into a reality. To Clare O'Loughlin for waving her design magic wand and turning my recipes into this beautiful cookbook. To Kim Rowney for putting up with my poor grammar and typos; your mind-blowing metric conversion skills on recipes is commendable! To Giuseppe Santamaria for spending a full day taking gorgeous portraits of me and making me look ten times younger!

To Kate Andrews, Josh Beggs, Phuoc Huynh, Penny Cai, Janine Sang, Heather Rudd, Elaine Tan, Stuart Muangsin, Sneh Roy, Melissa Young, Charisse Bough and Lisa Reed for being awesome recipe testers and sharing your honest feedback.

Last but not least, to all my friends in Sydney and around the world, thank you for following my gastronomic journey through my blog and cheering me on in MasterChef, you guys rock!

Published in 2012 by Hardie Grant Books

Hardie Grant Books (Australia), Ground Floor, Building 1 658 Church Street
Richmond, Victoria 3121, www.hardiegrant.com.au

Hardie Grant Books (UK) Dudley House, North Suite 34–35 Southampton Street
London WC2E 7HF, www.hardiegrant.co.uk

A Cataloguing-in-Publication entry is available from the
National Library of Australia

ISBN 9781742703817

Publishing director: Paul McNally
Editor: Kim Rowney
Design manager: Heather Menzies
Designer: Clare O'Loughlin
Food photographer and stylist: Billy Law
Additional photography: Giuseppe Santamaria
Production: Penny Sanderson

Colour reproduction by Splitting Image Colour Studio
Printed and bound in China by 1010 Printing International Limited